MW00895297

JOYFULLY
ENTER
THE TEMPLE

"We give ultimate thanks to God for how He has used Toni Pearson's powerful God-inspired gift of poetry to enrich our souls with spiritual insight and wisdom for everyday living. Your heart will be filled with praise as you meditate on God's word through Toni's eyes, and her beautiful poems and prayers in *Joyfully Enter the Temple*."

Reverend Norman and Dr. Cheryl Robinson
Fort Washington, Maryland

"*Joyfully Enter the Temple* manages to confront, comfort, console and empower...all in one book! Toni Carter Pearson transfers her spirituality through warm and compelling vignettes. Incorporating upfront sister-speak, she conveys insightful and inspirational samplings of life that anyone can relate to. My daily readings from *Joyfully Enter the Temple* are akin to my sending loving postcards to my soul. A must read for everyone. Thanks, Toni."

Lorene K. Robinson, Director of Alumni Affairs
Delaware State University - Dover, Delaware

"*Joyfully Enter the Temple* is a provocative book that helps an individual gain deeper insight into God, whether through meditation or through praise. The powerful poems written by this author, along with supporting scripture, encourage as well as empower believers into doing the will of God. My congregation and I use this book as part of our weekly worship. I would encourage others to do the same. This book is a must-read for all who love the Lord."

Reverend Sinclair Grey III, Pastor and Founder
The Liberation Temple - Mount Rainier, Maryland

"Ms. Pearson, it was indeed a part of God's plan for us to meet and for me to be blessed with the words from your book. As I started to read *Joyfully Enter the Temple*, I cried and felt so overwhelmed with joy and God's love. Thank you for writing this most inspiring book. It will continue to be a blessing to me as I embrace the journey God has for my life, everyday of my life! THANK YOU LORD!!"

Ms. Frances M. Dorsey
Washington, DC

JOYFULLY ENTER THE TEMPLE

Praise and Meditation Starters

To Carol,

Wishing you joy,

Soror Toni Carter Pearson

2017

TONI CARTER PEARSON

Dove & Turtle
PUBLISHING

FORT WASHINGTON, MARYLAND

Joyfully Enter the Temple

© 2004 by Toni Carter Pearson

Published by
Dove & Turtle Publishing
Post Office Box 44139
Fort Washington, MD 20749
E-mail: DoveandTurtle@aol.com

Cover Design and Logo by
JP Graphics & Promotional Design
5231-E Memorial Drive, Suite 232
Stone Mountain, GA 30038
E-mail: jpgraphics.inc@comcast.net

Published in the United States of America

First Printing 2004

ISBN: 0-9716271-2-6

LCCN: 2003096923

To roads leading home and joyful reunions.

C O N T E N T S

x

FOREWORD

*J*oyfully Enter the Temple: Praise and Meditation Starters* is such a novel idea. When I read it and observed how it all began because of the inspiration the author received from the computer E-mail talk between friends, I was amazed. But not so much so when I realized that the author's friend was also my daughter in ministry who had interned at our church for about three years. Under my leadership as pastor she was licensed and ordained to the gospel ministry.

Reverend Bessie Luticia Taylor Jett, lovingly known to me as "Tish," has certainly exemplified the teachings she received at the Way of the Cross Baptist Church in Kents Store, Virginia, where I serve as Pastor. Tish's dynamic strong love of God, her willingness to serve in the role as a servant in leading others to Jesus the Christ, and her determination to keep individuals from being spiritually lost are impressive. I am sure these outstanding traits were among the reasons she was called to serve as Pastor of the Esbie Baptist Church in Strasburg, Virginia.

I am comforted, filled with laughter, and overjoyed when almost every week I receive a call from Tish. She never forgets to thank me and the members of our congregation for what she says, "You've done for me." We feel that Tish blessed us, not only with her spirituality, but also her thoughtfulness, her outstanding ability, her God-given gifts, her spiritual laughter, and her love for people.

Tish has always stated to me that she wanted to have everything that God has for her. She is one person who never gives up, rarely ever seems to tire, always willing to accept a task, and unwilling to stop until it is well done.

Whenever Tish contacts me, she usually begins by saying, "I just needed a hug from you today." There is always one thing that I praise God for where Tish is concerned, and that is she is not ashamed to let others know that she occasionally has problems just as every human being does, but is willing to always praise God in every situation. I admire this in Tish.

I am most grateful to God to have Tish, Reverend Jett, as a daughter in the ministry. She has been called to provide servant leadership to others of God's children and I feel certain that they will not ever hunger for a piece of bread -- spiritual bread!

I say thanks to this author, Toni Carter Pearson, who has taken the *E-talk* she shared with Reverend Jett and put it to excellent use in *Joyfully Enter the Temple: Praise and Meditation Starters*. She is to be congratulated for her selection of Bible verses and for demonstrating through her poetry and devotions how we can live by them.

REVEREND DR. NAN M. BROWN

PREFACE

This book came into being because of the inspiration I received from the computer E-mail messages sent to me by a friend.

Reverend Bessie Luticia Jett and I became friends when we met in the ninth grade in high school. Our lives have taken different paths over the years, but our friendship has remained constant. We have managed to stay in touch and to support each other through many of our life experiences.

As an ordained minister, Reverend Jett dons her robes and preaches the gospel of Jesus Christ from her pulpit at Esbie Baptist Church in Strasburg, Virginia.

Over the past several years, Reverend Jett's full schedule of tasks associated with her marriage, her ministry, and her job, combined with my frequent job-related travel kept us from visiting each other as often as we would have liked. So we communicated by phone when we could, but we primarily stayed in touch through computer E-mail messages.

We *E-talk* about daily events, friends and family, the past, pressing concerns--about anything that happens to cross our minds. Sometimes it includes heavy conversations with snippets of prayer; other times it is pretty much the kind of gabbing and laughing we shared when we were teenagers.

Spirituality and the glory of Christ are part of every message. If we start out sharing notes about something funny, Reverend Jett manages to give the spiritual lesson that can be derived from that humorous event. If the topic is one of sadness or the day has been a little less than heartwarming, she can speak of the melancholy in terms that provide a glimpse of joy in that storm.

I used excerpts from various notes that she sent to me, selected scripture that relates to the basic idea of the excerpt, and let the LORD's will and word have free reign over my soul...*and keyboard*...when I sat down to write this book.

I am grateful for Reverend Jett's friendship and pleased to have witnessed her achievement of one milestone after another in pursuit of her calling. Through all of her hard work, her focus on the ministry over the years, her titles, and degrees, to me she has been simply, *Tish*, my friend.

ACKNOWLEDGMENTS

I joyfully acknowledge and extend my gratitude to those people who in one way or another, whether they knew it or not, were helpful to me in creating this book.

Above all others, I humbly thank my LORD and Savior Jesus Christ for life, family, friends, salvation, the gifts He chose for me, and His grace.

To my mother and late father, Helen and Clarke Carter; my sister, Barbara Wilks; my brother, Mark Carter; and other members of my family who have contributed in various ways to the person I have become, know that I love each of you dearly.

To Reverend Larry Collins and his wife Claudia, proprietors of the incredibly charming Inn, *Claudia's Manor Bed and Breakfast,* a southern mansion located in Savannah, Georgia, I am so appreciative of your warm hospitality during the Christmas holidays of 2000. Thank you for "birthing" a business that provides a peaceful haven and nurtured at least one aspiring writer.

I adore my Fort Foote Baptist Church family in Fort Washington, Maryland. To my pastor, Reverend Joseph W. Lyles, thank you for your "real-deal" preaching style, your wise counsel, and for exhibiting the light of Christ in your demeanor. To his wife, my friend, Sheila Lyles, thank you for your gentle spirit of friendship and for being my anchor more times than you could ever know. Thanks also to the members of the Women in Touch Ministry for your consistent display of unity, your humility, and most assuredly your devotion to God's purpose. To Marcie Swilley Washington, who (unknown to her until she reads this) gave me that definitive push to get on with this book when as a conference speaker she said to those of us sitting in her audience, "If you are not using the gifts...the talents...God gave you; if you are not doing what you know He called you to do, you are not being trustworthy." Thank you for getting my attention! To so many others not named here, thank you for blessing me with your words of encouragement and your Sunday morning hugs.

To the wonderfully talented Kelly Johnson, owner of *JP Graphics & Promotional Design* in Stone Mountain, Georgia, thank you for taking my rather obscure, often flaky ideas and creating wonderful designs for my dreams anyway. I am thrilled with your concepts for the cover of this book and my logo. You captured my vision.

To Reverend Dr. Nan M. Brown, Kevin Wayne Johnson, and Reverend Cessar Scott, thank you for agreeing, without hesitation, to my request to review and critique my manuscript. Your kind notes and contributions in the form of endorsements and the Foreword for this book are incredible blessings.

I am truly blessed to have a circle of special friends who pray for me, encourage me, check on me, advise me and stay close to me. To Myra Ashley, George Harris, DeEdwin Hursey, Jeff and Andrea Ledbetter, George Sherrod, Gloria Wallace, James Williams, and Dr. Anthony Yancey, thank you for your unselfish, kind and loving friendship.

Last but certainly not least, to Tish, thank you for sharing and caring for so many years. Your faith has strengthened mine. *Be blessed, my sistah...I'll catch you on the 'Net!*

INTRODUCTION

The theme of this book is joy--joy in the best of times, joy in the midst of storms, cup-runneth-over-and-sounding-of-the-trumpets joy, joy in the name of the LORD! The lessons taught here are about displaying your joy through praise, and summoning your joy through meditation.

The passages used are excerpts from various E-mail messages Reverend Bessie L. Jett sent to me during a three-year period. I chose them because they are not from her sermons, but are simply conversations. They are the words that she shared at points in time when she was feeling on top of the world or found herself in an emotional valley; when she was joyous, or near tears. Some of them show her in a relaxed mood while at other times she is dismayed over health issues of family and friends. You will read things she wrote to soothe my worried soul or just to provide me with a laugh when I needed it. She also wrote of her concern for others or told me how she wrapped herself in the safety net of the Holy Spirit as she was preparing for worship. She described times when she felt particularly vulnerable, or helped others to keep negative situations and people from influencing their lives.

Many of the thoughts Reverend Jett shared in her notes reminded me of particular scriptures, or caused me to go to the Bible to get a spiritual basis. Because of what she wrote and the scriptures that I found in the Bible, my own personal journal became a repository for random thoughts, phrases and ideas that I eventually expanded into the poems, devotions and prayers that make up this book.

In Reverend Jett's words you will find your own. She has some of the same thoughts you have had, emotions you have felt, frustrations you have endured. Sometimes she struggles with knowing how to deal with life on an earthly level, but she always knows how to find the answers on a spiritual level.

Often we tend to put ministers on a pedestal and forget that they sometimes have valley moments just as the rest of us do. But the reality is that they, too, live lives which provide testimonies. Indeed, many times the men and women who are our shepherds can provide us with eloquent sermons and Godly advice, based not on what they have heard, but on the joys and pains from their own experiences.

My hope is that *Joyfully Enter the Temple* will serve as a reminder that as a child of God, from time to time every person (even those who have been called to preach the Christian gospel from a pulpit) faces challenges, uncertainties, and stresses. And at those times, more than ever, no matter what our calling, we need the joy of the LORD. This book is designed to help you focus on that joy, and to let you know that particular events can be cause for either praise or meditation, or on occasion, both.

Each of the "*Starters*" consists of three parts: (1) an excerpt from Reverend Jett's E-mail message, (2) one or more Bible verses, and (3) a poem, prayer or devotion.

Use the words of Reverend Jett as a testimony to your everyday life or for a particular situation you have encountered.

Study the scriptures included here as a foundation for renewing and steadying your Christian walk.

Immerse yourself in the poetry, the prayers, and the devotions that God placed on my heart and allow them to ignite the flame in your spirit, to open up a space in your soul in which to offer praise. Or reflect on them in order to gain focus for your periods of meditation.

"As a deer thirsts for streams of water," (*Psalms 42:1, NCV*), so should we all thirst for the word of God and the words from God to spur us on during quiet meditation or when singing praises to Him, and finding joy in doing so. In whatever way you choose to revere, honor, celebrate or communicate with the Heavenly Father, do it joyfully…in the name of the LORD.

JOYFULLY ENTER THE TEMPLE

How do we behold His blessings?
How do we thank Him enough?
How do we keep our faith in check when things in our lives get tough?

It all is so very simple,
we just joyfully enter the temple.

This joy does not have to be laughter,
a chuckle, a giggle or smile.
It is the soothing warmth we feel down in our soul
Just by knowing His word is worthwhile.

How do we get over the sorrow?
How do we remove the pain?
How do we stop the tears that fall from our eyes like a driving rain?

It all is so very simple,
we just joyfully enter the temple.

This temple is not a building,
it is neither a room nor a place.
It is His presence and our frame of mind
We must have to give God His grace.

How do we reach Him with our praise?
How do we meditate on His glory?
How do we phrase our testimony to share with others His story?

It all is so very simple,
we just joyfully enter the temple.

...And in this place I will bring peace.
I, the LORD almighty, have spoken!
Haggai 2:9
(NLT)

"Hi Toni,

... This has been on my mind for a while. I'm listening hard to any message from the LORD. I would like to have more time to spend on my ministry--I look forward to the time where I can just spend all days with the LORD, studying the word and meditating on it, reading my books.

Be blessed.

Tish"

SPENDING TIME

Genesis 5:24, 6:9

*And Enoch
walked
with God...*

*...and Noah
walked
with God...*
(KJV)

To awaken one morning and know that I
Will spend the whole day with the LORD
To talk, to share, to laugh, to cry
And dwell on His holy word.

To point to a tree and thank Him
For its leaves and the sky above
To show Him how much it means to me
That He gave me this world out of love.

To quietly whisper in His ear
And tell Him what is in my soul
To thank Him for spending this day so near
Helping to keep me whole.

But I need not wish for a special day
The LORD is always right there
When I rise each morning and begin to pray
He already knows my prayer.

So no matter what my schedule may say
No matter what jobs I must do
I know that the LORD is with me each day
Guiding me, seeing me through.

"... Same old, same old! ..."

THE NEXT PAGE

Okay, so yesterday was not exactly as expected.
And none of us has a clue about tomorrow.
All we have, with a measure of certainty,
is what God has put before us today.

Lamentations 3:21-23

*But I have hope
when I think of this:
The LORD's love
never ends;
his mercies
never stop.
They are new
every morning.
(NCV)*

We may think each of our days is the same,
but they really are not. Every day is different.
Every day is a renewal of God's grace and
our spirit...a freshness to enhance our lives.

Each day we are given a new life page on
which to record our story for that day.
The page may look empty, but it is full of the
word and blessings of God when we receive it.

Each of us must take that new page and design
a day that is pleasing in the sight of the Father.

John 8:25

*Then said they
unto him,
Who art thou?
And Jesus saith
unto them,
Even the same
that I said unto you
from the beginning.
(KJV)*

What God gave yesterday was for yesterday.
Today He has a whole new list of mercies to
adorn our lives.

We must take it, add to it the blessings He
gives us, throw in a bit of His grace, the
promises of Jesus Christ and the protection
of the Holy Spirit.

Each day the God who watches over us is the
same God who has always watched over us.

Only God is the same.

Only God.

"... But abundant blessings are mine just for the asking and I'm learning to ask. ..."

1 Chronicles 4:9-10

There was a man named Jabez...
(NLT)
And Jabez called on the God of Israel, saying,
"Oh, that you would bless me indeed, and enlarge my territory,
and that your hand would be with me,
and that you would keep me from evil,
that I may not cause pain!"
So God granted him what he requested.
(NKJV)

Matthew 6:8

... for your Father knoweth what things ye have need of,
before ye ask him.
(KJV)

Luke 11:10

For every one that asketh receiveth;
and he that seeketh findeth;
and to him that knocketh it shall be opened.
(KJV)

James 1:6

But let him ask in faith, nothing wavering.
For he that wavereth is like a wave of the sea
driven with the wind and tossed.
(KJV)

JUST ASK, ANYWAY

The blessed, gracious, merciful Father in heaven will always provide your needs. The one thing that He requires is that you ask for what you desire.

If you want His guidance you need to ask for it. If you want His direction you need to tell Him where you're trying to go and ask for His help in getting there. If you want God's protection, tell Him what you fear and ask Him to shelter you. If you feel you're moving toward temptation, ask Him to keep you on His path. If you find yourself falling, ask Him to let you lean on Him.

God is just waiting to shower you with more blessings than you could ever imagine. But He wants to keep the lines of communication open. Let Him hear your request and your reasons for that request. Tell Him exactly what you desire. Believe that He will provide it. He already knows what you want, what you need, what has been earmarked only for you. But if He gave it freely without your having asked first, then perhaps you might become complacent and not feel the need to ask.

You might take Him for granted because you know that without even making an effort, you're going to get what you want *anyway*. You might forget the need for prayer, because such petitions would seem a waste of time when what you want is going to be given *anyway*. The Bible might become less important in your life, because you'll not feel the need to armor yourself with His holy word since He's going to protect you *anyway*.

You might mistakenly begin to believe that the power and strength He gives you to survive hard times are not from Him but are of your own doing. You might see your brother or sister, not as someone who has equal footing with you as a child of the King, but instead as someone having lower status than you...someone not worthy of your attention.

And eventually, the light of Christ that shines in those who know from whence cometh their help, will no longer shine in you, because without having asked Him for the power that keeps that light shining, your little flame of faith will burn out forever.

So keep in touch with Him, ask Him to help you, even when you know the blessing is coming *anyway*. And above all else, remember that He is the answer in ***every way***.

"... I just must remember, that I represent the LORD Jesus Christ. I have to strive to always do my best to His glory, even here. The LORD had placed me in this place and I figured it was for me to develop some fruit -- patience, tolerance, long suffering. ..."

ONLY THE BEST WILL DO

Daniel 2:22

...he knoweth what is in the darkness, and the light dwelleth with him. (KJV)

If where you are doesn't suit you,
a place that's not all you wish,
Remember that Jesus Christ still expects
the very best from us.

Take a good look around you,
and find the spirit there
Remember that Christ, the LORD,
did not find joy everywhere.

Jonah 2:2

``In my great trouble I cried to the Lord and he answered me; from the depths of death I called, and Lord, you heard me! (TLB)

Like Daniel, just keep looking forward,
Like Jonah, just shout out His name;
Like the woman who touched the hem of His robe,
She never again was the same.

We don't always know God's purpose,
Perhaps that's the way it should be;
But He is the author of the master plan
To get the best from you and me.

Mark 5:28

For she said, If I may touch but his clothes, I shall be whole. (KJV)

You're only here for a very short time,
so make your stay worthwhile
Bring glory to wherever you happen to be,
if only with a smile.

"... It hit me and my spirits were low...I was in the valley for a moment but I praise God that everything is alright now. Above every valley is a testimony to God and my faith in Him. Praise the LORD - Ok, I feel my help coming so I can move forward now. ..."

PEACE IN EVERY VALLEY

I.   You've been praying, going to church, studying the Bible, talking to the LORD. But things aren't going quite right in your life. You feel as if you have lost your joy. People often speak of those times as valley moments. You look at valley moments as being bad times, times when you are down, times when so much in your life seems to be going wrong. You look around you and just don't see the beauty anywhere. It all looks and feels so bleak. You think, "Surely God didn't mean for me to be here. Surely this low point, this valley in my life, is not His doing."   And all you want to do at that point is shout, cry out for His perfect strength to enfold you in this valley.

II.   You've been saving, budgeting for months, all for this moment. This vacation. There you are standing on the edge, peering down into a valley--the Grand Canyon. You're in awe; your spirit is filled. You are anxiously awaiting the arrival of your guide so that you can venture down into that valley, because you know that only God could have produced the beauty you see below you. Once you're all the way down in that valley you feel the spirit of God move through you just as if He were right there standing with you holding your hand. And all you want to do at that point is shout, cry out for His perfect strength to enfold you in this valley.

Luke 3:5

Every valley shall be filled, and every mountain and hill shall be brought low; and the crooked shall be made straight, and the rough ways shall be made smooth; (KJV)

Pondering valleys

Which valley do you suppose is of God?
Do you think He wants us in one valley and not the other?
Do you think He's with us in one valley and not the other?
Can you find God's purpose in the first valley?
If you didn't experience the first valley,
could you appreciate the second?
Do you expect that anything other than the mercy and goodness of God could bring you safely out of either valley?

Pray for God's presence and deliverance in both valleys.

OYFULLY ENTER THE TEMPLE

"... She has finally acknowledged--out loud--what she has known in her
heart for some time. I knew the LORD was calling her. I could see the
signs, but she just wasn't ready to accept it. She's waiting for further
instructions, since her ministry will be different from mine. The LORD
told her. So I'll sit back and watch her bloom. ..."

Jeremiah 1:17

Therefore prepare yourself and arise,
and speak to them all that I command you.
(NKJV)

Mark 4:20
And these are they which are sown on good ground;
such as hear the word, and receive it, and bring forth fruit,
some thirtyfold, some sixty, and some an hundred.
(KJV)

Romans 12:6-7

Having then gifts differing according to the grace that is given to us,
whether prophecy, let us prophesy according to the proportion of faith;
Or ministry, let us wait on our ministering:
or he that teacheth, on teaching;
(KJV)

1 Timothy 4:6

If you instruct the brethren in these things, you will be a good minister
of Jesus Christ, nourished in the words of faith and of the
good doctrine which you have carefully followed.
(NKJV)

HOW IS YOUR HEARING?

The LORD calls each of us to a different ministry.

Ministry is a way of using our gifts and talents to help others know God.
It is using an endowment to conduct ourselves in such a way that others will
see God's goodness in us, and thereby be moved to revere Him and
worship Him.

Your ministry may be a calling to the pulpit, whereas mine may not have
me donning the robes of a worship leader. Those to whom He has given
that calling are very few indeed. My ministry might be a special knack with
gardening, where I could use my abilities to provide a needy neighbor with
fresh vegetables, or a nursing home with colorful flowers. But each ministry
is a special gift from God. Each has equal importance in His sight. Each
provides the opportunity to let others know of His grace and mercy.

He provides us with gifts, makes them known to us, and then allows us to put
them to use. He stands back and watches how we develop the gift, how we
hone our talents and creativity to put it to the best use for His glory, how we
use who we are and whose we are to help others know that
God is in us, God is in them, God is.

Whatever ministry the LORD has chosen especially for each of us, we should
always be appreciative of it, nurture and use it fully to glorify and honor
His name.

Do you know what your ministry is? What are you hearing from the LORD?
Are you really listening for His word? What is your heartfelt desire?
What is the one thing you believe you should be doing but aren't?
What is it that you feel you must do?

Listen and be ready to hear.
Hear and be ready to do.
Do and be blessed.

"... My friends down south are going through some troubling times right now. My prayer partners and I have been standing in the gap and we're in serious prayer for him and his wife. I would like to be able to visit them now, but I can't get away at this time. The LORD knows my heart. ..."

Romans 10:1

Brethren,
my heart's desire
and prayer to God
...is, that they
might be saved.
(KJV)

Acts 4:31-32

After this prayer,
the building where
they were meeting
shook and they were
all filled with the
Holy Spirit and
boldly preached
God's message.
All the believers
were of one heart
and mind, and no
one felt that what he
owned was his own;
everyone was
sharing.
(TLB)

STANDING IN THE GAP

Dear Father we stand in this circle of prayer,
May the words we speak reach your throne.
There are worries, hard times,
and concerns, Dear LORD
Suddenly touching two of your own.

We know he bowed down
and asked for your touch.
We heard as she prayed through the day.
But LORD we know that they need us as well
To stand in the gap to pray.

The enemy came by to crush their faith
At a moment when they weren't strong.
But your armor we wear, God,
and this circle is tight,
To show Satan his timing is wrong.

We know their deliverance is in your hands,
Father, we'll stand with them day-by-day.
As you test their faith,
you strengthen our hearts,
So we stand in the gap and pray.

"... Whatever way the LORD chooses to heal me, it's alright with me 'cause I know He will heal. God is good, and I feel my help coming on. I'm going to get better. I am so appreciative of the angels stationed around me to protect me. ..."

Jeremiah 17:14

LORD, heal me
and, I will truly
be healed.
Save me
and I will truly
be saved.
You are the one
I praise.
(NCV)

Psalms 91:11-12

For he shall give
his angels
charge over thee,
to keep thee
in all thy ways.
They shall bear thee
up in their hands,
lest thou dash thy foot
against a stone.
(KJV)

CARED FOR BY THE GREATEST PHYSICIAN

You know what is ailing me, O LORD,
You know just how I feel;
The things that are causing pain within
I'll wait for you to heal.

The doctors I've seen have examined me,
All of them trying their best;
They prescribe all sorts of pills to take
Or recommend more tests.

But your angels are posted by my side,
They're surrounding my doctors too;
And we all know that the healing will come
In due time, with a word from you.

Thank you dear LORD, for I shall be healed,
Thank you for saving me;
However you choose to heal me now
Will be my testimony.

"... The LORD is preparing you for a blessing and has to remove that which you cannot remove so you will have more love to give to Him and a wonderful testimony to share with others. ..."

Isaiah 61:11

For as the earth bringeth forth her bud, and as the garden causeth the things that are sown in it to spring forth; so the LORD GOD will cause righteousness and praise to spring forth...
(KJV)

Psalms 1:3

And he shall be like a tree planted by the rivers of water, that bringeth forth his fruit in his season; his leaf also shall not wither; and whatsoever he doeth shall prosper.
(KJV)

IN HIS GARDEN

I am planted in a garden
to grow, to flower, to bloom.
Tended by the gardener,
Nourished by the groom.

My soul grows in His goodness,
Feet rooted in His best soil,
He cares for me and others too;
With us He'll gently toil.

And when my leaves are wilted
He gently starts to prune,
To take away the things that hurt
Or spoil my life too soon.

He gives me strength to bear his fruit
Adds love to make it sweet;
I'll blossom forth with testimony
To share with all I meet.

"... I told him that if God has set a schedule for him to make that move, has set the season for him, then anytime is the right time 'cause when God hits you, you will definitely move. ..."

SEASONS

God has a plan of
empowerment and salvation
for each of us.

Acts 1:7-8

*And he said unto
them, It is not for you
to know the times
or the seasons,
which the Father
hath put in his own
power. But ye shall
receive power,
after that the
Holy Ghost is
come upon you
(KJV)*

Some parts of the plan
He lets us control,
other parts of the plan
He issues forth to us
according to His own schedule.

If we do well with the part
He gives us to control,
we are guided toward
the rest of His plan.

If we are prepared,
and act in accordance
with His will,
then we will know
when the time is right.

Isaiah 50:4

*The LORD God
hath given me the
tongue of the learned,
that I should know
how to speak a word
in season
to him that is weary:
(KJV)*

If we are unprepared,
or put off what we know
we are supposed to do
in His name, then the time
is not right.

Jesus promises us that we shall
benefit from His power.

It is up to us to listen carefully
and be aware of the season
appointed by the Father,
not the date on the calendar
nor the hour on the clock.

"... I didn't get to this point in my life in the way I expected to. There have been some twists and turns, and as you know, a bump or two in the road along the way. But I like where I am. I'm grateful, in a very quiet way and so thankful to God for the journey. ..."

MY JOURNEY

For years I made choices, my goals I set,
And with little thought, my journey I planned.
Without a prayer, I started on my way
And often wound up in sinking sand.

Ecclesiastes 9:17

*The words of
wise men
are heard
in quiet
more
than the cry
of him that
ruleth
among fools.*
(KJV)

I looked at the things I had done in my life
And decided that I wanted a change.
I had not always lived according to God's will,
My missteps and mistakes were plain.

Angry and frustrated I chided myself;
There was really no one else I could blame.
I had chosen not to listen, not to pray, not to wait;
So of course God's counsel never came.

My plans for my journey, I put aside,
I prayed and asked God to show me His way;
"Yell at me, scream at me,
whatever you wish LORD,
Just order my steps today."

Genesis 24:21

*And the man,
wondering at her,
remained silent
so as to know
whether the LORD
had made his journey
prosperous
or not.
(NKJV)*

I paced and listened for His voice to boom,
To fill the air with a thunderous roar.
But that's not His way, I knew all along
He would whisper as He had done before.

So I calmed myself, and praised His name
Quietly asked God with my heart sincere,
to lead me, guide me, show me the way
that I may reach His path from here.

I do not know what is ahead of me
But I know there is nothing to fear.
My heart whispers hallelujah
At God's gentle voice in my ear.

"... I have joy, joy, joy, joy, down in my heart for Jesus is my king and he is blessing me. ..."

OH, JOY, JOY, JOY, JOY

John 15:11

These things have I spoken unto you that my joy might remain in you, and that your joy might be full.
(KJV)

1 Peter 1:8

You love him even though you have never seen him. Though you do not see him, you trust him; and even now, you are happy with a glorious, inexpressible joy
(NLT)

What is joy?
Do you really know
joy?
The joy of God
is unlike any other kind of
pleasure we could ever have.
We speak of it as being in our heart,
but if you open a heart
you would not find
this thing we call
joy.
God, Jesus, the Holy Spirit
all give us joy;
these invisible forces of
power and love
bless us with this thing called
joy.
Can you see them putting it before you,
handing you something you cannot
touch or feel, but knowing anyway
to the depth of your soul that it is so real?
The source of joy is always God.
We don't create it ourselves;
we experience it through serving Him and
developing a right relation with Him.
The fruit of living and
walking in the Spirit is
joy.

"... The LORD surely blessed me in a mighty way today with a subject REMEMBER and the LORD just gave me the words while I kept my finger pointed to the word 'remembrance' - Luke 22:19 - where they were getting ready to have communion and the LORD said this doeth in remembrance of me. The subject was REMEMBER but the question was what do you remember - good times, happy times, trials and tribulations and God was with you the entire time bringing you through - the LORD blessed, and I just let the LORD use me. ..."

Luke 22:19

...this do in remembrance
of me.
(KJV)

2 Timothy 2:8-9

Remember that Jesus Christ,
of the seed of David,
was raised from the dead
according to my gospel,
for which I suffer trouble
as an evildoer, even to the
point of chains; but the
word of God
is not chained.
(NKJV)

Psalms 20:7

...but we will remember
the name
of the LORD
our God.
(KJV)

REMEMBER

What do you remember?
What do you keep in mind?
Is it worth the effort?
Is it pleasure that you find?

Do you recall the good times?
Do they warm up your heart?
Or is it tribulations
That tear your days apart?

Do you give thanks for good days,
Knowing the LORD is there?
When things are bad do you remember
That you're still in His care?

Do you remember the book, His word?
Do you pick it up and read?
Do you fill your heart and mind
With the words of David's seed?

He blesses in a mighty way
Knows what you're going through;
Just trust and do remember
He's always there with you.

"... No one can stop the word of God coming forward from the sisters; and then you see Bishop Vashti, a Howard graduate, being used mightily for the LORD. Closed doors will open and those folks that remain closed, in my opinion, will be stifled from growth. The LORD IS in charge. ..."

NO DOUBT

It is not for me to say
that she is not going the right way.
It is not for me to ask
Why she struggles and gives all to this task.
It is not for me to ignore
As she goes on doing God's chore.
It is not for me to deny
That her faith is in abundant supply.

Proverbs 8:2, 3, 6, 7, 8

*She stands on the hilltop
and at the crossroads.
(NLT)
She crieth at the gates,
at the entry of the city,
at the coming in
at the doors.
Hear; for I will speak
Of excellent things;
and the opening
of my lips
shall be right things.
For my mouth
shall
speak truth;
... All the words
of my mouth
are in righteousness
...They are all plain
to him that
understandeth,
and right to
them that find
knowledge.
(KJV)*

I know what she's believed all her life,
*"Trust God, and avoid Satan's strife,
Go to church, learn of the LORD,
Read the Bible, study His word.
Tell others how He blesses your heart,
Call His name before troubles start;
Be loving and a kindhearted friend,
Be a light on whom others can depend."*

It is not for me to say,
"Only a man over me can pray."
It is not for me to ask,
"God, is hers a legitimate task?"
It is not for me to ignore
When she says, *"Trust God, avoid Satan's door."*
It is not for me to deny
That God gives her grace in abundant supply.

I don't believe God's plan has been broken;
Of His love and grace she has never misspoken.
I only know that I've heard her pray,
I've seen her walk in an upright way.
I watched her love those who would try
To make her turn back, and her calling deny.
His mercy is shown through her holy laughter,
As she promises to embrace Him forever after.

"... I preached to the youth, told them they need to be on their way upward not downward. As much as Satan wants to sift them and see what they're made of, go forward, follow God. They're young, don't think they're ever gonna die and some of them just rolled their eyes, but I think I reached most of them and if I didn't this time I'll just keep trying. I told them not to miss out on the rewards God has for them in His heavenly home. ..."

Matthew 13:43

The godly will shine like the sun in their Father's Kingdom.
Anyone who is willing to hear should listen and understand!
The Kingdom of Heaven is like a treasure...
(NLT)

1 Peter 1:13, 17-20

So think clearly and exercise self-control.
Look forward to the special blessings
that will come to you at the return of Jesus Christ.
And remember that the heavenly Father to whom you pray
has no favorites when He judges. He will judge or reward
you according to what you do. So you must live in reverent
fear of him during your time...here on earth. For you know that
God paid a ransom to save you from the empty life you inherited
from your ancestors. And the ransom he paid was not mere
gold or silver. He paid for you with the precious lifeblood of Christ,
the sinless, spotless Lamb of God. God chose him for this purpose
long before the world began...And he did this for you.
(NLT)

Hebrews 4:13

Nothing in all the world can be hidden from God. Everything is clear and lies
open before him, and to him we must explain the way we have lived.

THE MEETING

The appointment is made, your name is on the list; the registry has long been set.
I know that you know what is scheduled for you; but it's something one tries to forget.
You are wondering what I am talking about, but you know so well of the plan.
I speak of an hour unknown but a date not escaped by woman or man.
The time will come when you must take your turn, go home to meet the Master.
Each of us here must travel that road, to that place of forever after.
But just tell me this, when you arrive and meet God what are you going to say?
Have you ever rehearsed, chosen the best words, prepared at all for that day?
What? You have no speech, no memorized scripture, no polished prose to recite?
Then how do you know when you're there with Him
that your words will come out right?

Do you know just how you'll stand, what your body language will say?
Do you think it will matter right then in His presence that you're having a bad hair day?
Have you imagined what the place will look like? A throne, a desk, The Book?
Does He have a chair there for you to take a seat? Do you kneel or just stand and look?
Will He walk up to you, address you by name, or patiently wait for you to speak?
Will you boldly utter some gracious words, or just humble yourself, and be meek?
Will your voice have a booming prayer refrain, or a soft and spiritual chant?
Please promise me you won't high-five the Master and shout out in a hip-hop slant!
What can you say that He doesn't know? You can't bring Him good news from the 'hood.
He already knows you, watched you each day. Too late then to say you tried to do good!
Your smirk tells me that you're scheming right now,
thinking by then you'll have some idea
Of how best to spin the things that you've done, make it all what He wants to hear.
What? That's not working for you? You can't fix it up?
You can't make it sound quite right?
But you've been so good at deceit before. Didn't you just lie to someone last night?

I pray that by now you have come to realize that you will someday meet the Judge;
So please keep in mind as you prepare for that day there is nothing you can fudge.
With the time you have left be in preparation, make the effort to live life right;
See each moment, each day as precious; live by His word to be worthy in His sight.
You see, He may not ask for conversation, perhaps He won't speak a word;
But His presence and grace will bring sounds to your ears
unlike anything you've ever heard.
Do not be stubborn, let God in your heart. Sing a song to His mercy and power.
Because one day you, just like all of us here will arrive at that fateful hour.

"... I went to bed in need of a good cry and woke up this morning still in need of a good cry. So I went upstairs and laid before the LORD. And as the words poured from my lips, the tears flowed freely from my eyes. ..."

TEARDROPS AND TIMECLOCKS

Psalms 61:2-3

*From the end
of the earth
will I cry unto thee,
when my heart is
overwhelmed;
lead me to the rock
that is higher than I.
For thou has been
a shelter for me,
and a strong tower
from the enemy.
(KJV)*

Psalms 138:3

*In the day when I
cried out,
You answered me,
And made me bold
with strength
in my soul.
(NKJV)*

The joy of the LORD is an amazing,
exciting, wondrous experience.

There are times, however,
when circumstances bring sadness
to our spirit, when joy seemingly takes
a back seat to overwhelming heartache.

It can happen for a number of reasons--
when we see someone in trouble,
a loved one is ill or dies or leaves,
when our feelings are hurt, when finances
are not adequate, when there is difficulty
in a relationship or on the job.

Often, during those times, our internal
reaction to such events results in shedding
tears as a way of venting our frustrations.
It can happen as an uncontrollable episode,
or it can be as minor as a few tears
welling up in our eyes.

It is possible that the hurt can be so deep,
so traumatic that the joy is not back the
following morning as we look at
our calendars.

But joy does come back in the morning...
according to God's clock.
He is the One who determines how long
the night will be.

"... I called and told them I wanted to help them. We hadn't been in touch for a long while, but because they needed help I had to contact them. I think they may have doubted my motives at first. I know I'm not perfect but you know I try to represent the LORD Jesus Christ and I strive to always do my best to His glory. ..."

BOUND TO CHRIST

John 14:19-20

Yet a little while, and the world seeth me no more; but ye see me: because I live, ye shall live also. At that day ye shall know that I am in my Father, and ye in me, and I in you. (KJV)

John 14:26

But the Comforter, which is the Holy Ghost, whom the Father will send in my name, he shall teach you all things and bring all things to your remembrance, whatsoever I have said unto you. (KJV)

Many of us say we are striving for perfection, but the nature of human beings is to *not* be perfect.

We are all born in sin, so we start out with something less than perfection.

God did not design us to be perfect individuals, but rather as people who have the opportunity to make choices based on what we know about Him and His expectations for us.

He gave us free will. He expects our choices to be made in such a manner that we will be led to glorify Him.

Even if we stray away from our fellowship with God for a while, when we reach out to Him, He is always there.

Christ is no longer physically in our presence, but this does not mean that we should not strive to be like Him.

Through His miracles, parables, prayers and instructions, He left us explicit guidance on how to live.

And as an extra layer of protection, He provided the Holy Spirit so that our bond with Him will remain intact until He returns.

"... I've been trying to work my sermon around 'asking for forgiveness.'
Did you see the article in today's paper about the pastors? I know one of
them, and I know that he redeemed himself, admitted his faults to his church
and God AND himself, and really worked hard to get back on the right
track. He has a powerful testimony, and God is using him in a mighty way. I
heard him speak recently. See, you never read anything in the paper about
how they came through...only about how they went astray. ..."

Psalms 119:67

I used to wander off until you disciplined me;
but now I closely follow your word.
(NLT)

1 Peter 2:25

For ye were as sheep going astray;
but are now returned unto the
Shepherd and Bishop of your souls.
(KJV)

Luke 15:10

...there is joy in the presence of the angels of God
when one sinner changes his heart and life.
(NVC)

PAST...OR, PASTOR!

The hymns had been sung, collection collected,
the welcome and words of prayer had been said;
The pastor stood up with a message to give,
but decided to offer his testimony instead.
"Church, I grew up living my life for Christ and humbly answered His call to preach.
I stood in the pulpit and praised His name, but temptation crept within my reach.
So I was obedient to God on Sundays, attentive to my marriage after church.
I gave in to the world the other six days; on the prowl, for fun and sin I did search.
Oh, I asked the LORD to forgive me. Told myself life was rough, I was stressed;
But I knew in my soul, and so did God, that my lies were not words of the blessed.
I preached a good game from the pulpit; told others how to live Godly lives;
Then spent my time outside of church running after other husbands wives.
When my life started falling into shambles, I clutched onto the world even more;
I asked God to help me through these bad times; but I kept sinning as much as before.
Don't you know I blamed the bad stuff on others?
Wouldn't admit why my life was going astray;
I was much too deep in sin to face the reality
That God loved me and was putting signs in my way.
I shunned the signs so God took His arms from around me,
He released me, let me stand on my own;
My worldly ways broke the fellowship I had with Him;
Depression and turmoil cut me to the bone.
I was unhappy with all those around me;
Preparing sermons and doing ministry was a chore;
Sick of my marriage, disgusted with my home...
Church, when God lets you go, nothing's as it was before.
Finally my life got so bad I hit bottom.
I saw the worst of myself without Christ;
Realized the world had nothing good to offer me,
Folks, because I dishonored God, I paid the price.
I know, some of you were shocked that He got my attention;
Some of you prayed while others threw up their hands;
But believers, as you know, when we ask and are sincere,
God will change our worldly ways to heavenly plans.
I'm here today, assuredly a new creature in Christ.
Years have passed, but church, I'll never forget,
That God loved me, family forgave me, you took me back;
After all this time I still can't thank Him enough yet.
So remember, we all are nothing more than human,
Can slip and fall even if it's a pastor's robe we wear.
But God will pick us up, wrap His loving arms around us,
And, hallelujah, all it takes is faith and prayer."
I left church that day with joy in my soul,
meditated on the preacher's words as I drove along.
I praised my Savior for testimony that soothed my spirit
and placed in my heart a triumphant song.

"... After prayer service ended and everyone had gone, I locked the church doors and strutted my usher steps all around the sanctuary singing our songs - boy did I have a great time. ..."

Psalms 98:4

Make a joyful noise unto the LORD, all the earth: make a loud noise, and rejoice, and sing praise. (KJV)

Psalms 47:1-2

Oh, clap your hands, all you peoples! Shout to God with the voice of triumph! For the LORD Most High is awesome... (NKJV)

1 Thessalonians 4:16

For the LORD himself will descent from Heaven with a shout...and with the trumpet of God. (NKJV)

.

SHARING MY JOY WITH ME

Every now and then
you find that you
just can't
sit down on God.

You have to get up,
move about,
let your voice be heard,
even if there is no one
there to hear it but you.

Shouting for the Savior
does not mean you have to be
in the midst of a crowd;
it simply means
you have to be
in the midst
of the Savior

"... I cried tears of thanksgiving. ..."

THANKFUL

Many times you can be so overwhelmed by all your blessings that you can't even voice the words *thank you.*

Isaiah 25:8

...And the LORD God will wipe away tears from all faces.
(NKJV)

When you look around and take note of all you have been given by God, with so little required of you, sometimes you can do nothing more than shed the tears of thanksgiving. Sometimes, tears are all you can offer to show your gratitude.

Psalms 119:145

I cried with my whole heart;
hear me, O LORD:
(KJV)

But that is okay. Tears are okay. You don't have to shout out the words *thank you* in order for the Father to know you are grateful. You can let the depth of your emotion relay to God how you feel about all He has done for you. He will know the reason for your tears, will know that they are a sign of your heartfelt thanks.

Psalms 88:2

Let my prayer come before thee:
incline thine ear unto my cry;
(KJV)

The emotion that comes with knowing we all have been given this amazing gift of life, can sometimes make you feel that *thank you* isn't enough.

To realize that we have been chosen to receive all that God has to offer.

...WOW!

"... I see a cloud coming and I've started shouting and sending up praises. ..."

CLARITY IN THE CLOUDS

Clouds are part of an ever-changing life.

You cannot keep them away,
but you can brace yourself for them.

Genesis 9:13

*I set my rainbow
in the cloud
and it shall be
for the sign
of the covenant
between Me
and the earth.
(NKJV)*

Start your shouting early;
send up your praises well ahead of time.

When you look around you and sense
that trouble is coming, send up praises.

If upcoming situations are causing you stress,
start shouting.

Offer thanks to the Father for being by your
side when clouds surround you.

Luke 9:35

*And there came a voice
out of the cloud,
saying,
This is my beloved Son:
hear him.
(KJV)*

You know He is going to bring you through it.

You can never start praising Him too early.

Clouds contain rainbows which are a sign
of God's covenant to us.

Look for the rainbow in those cloudy situations.

There is some good in every cloud filled event.

Look for the lesson
that God wants you to get
from the clouds.

"... Had a great day today - preached without shoes - got so out there for the LORD at altar prayer I kicked them off. ..."

FAITH FASHION

Luke 22:35

*And he said unto them,
When I sent you
without purse,
and scrip,
and shoes,
lacked ye any thing?
And they said,
Nothing.
(KJV)*

Proverbs 31:25

*Strength and honor
are her clothing...
(KJV)*

Isaiah 59:17

*For he put on righteousness
as a breastplate,
and an helmet of salvation
upon his head;
and he put on the garments
of vengeance for clothing,
and was clad with zeal
as a cloak.
(KJV)*

The LORD is not concerned
about how you're clothed
on the outside
when you praise
Him.
What He looks for is
how you're clothed
on the inside.

What covering
is your heart wearing?
Is it wrapped in warmth
or hardened with an icy chill?

How fashionably dressed
is your humility?
Is there simplicity and
modesty in your essence?

Is your spirit
properly adorned
with love and praise
for Him?

Have you accessorized
the substance of your soul
with kindness to your fellow man?

God doesn't look for shoes
when you lift your voice to Him.
He looks for sincerity.

Whether in your secret closet
or surrounded by others at altar prayer
God only looks for your garment of faith...
your cloak that reflects the warmth of
His grace.

"... I was determined to worship and I did. I wasn't about to let Satan get in my way. ..."

Matthew 4:8-11

*Satan...showed him the
nations of the world
and all their glory.
"I'll give it all to you,"
he said, "if you will only
kneel and worship me."
"Get out of here, Satan",
Jesus told him. "The
Scriptures say, 'Worship
only the LORD God. Obey
only him.'" Then Satan
went away...
(TLB)*

Zechariah 3:2

*And the LORD said to
Satan, "I have decreed
mercy to Joshua..."
(TLB)*

James 5:11

*Job is an example of a
man who continued to
trust the LORD in sorrow.
(TLB)*

MESSAGE TO SATAN

You cannot stop my walk with God,
Can't interrupt my praise;
I'll worship Him with all my heart,
Magnify Him through all my days.

I know your tricks, your lures, your lies,
Heard you say your way is best.
You promise me a bright, shiny world,
But God gives me a life that's blessed.

You tried but you could not tempt Jesus;
He told us what you said.
You also tried with Joshua and Job,
But they, too, followed God instead.

I'm striving for a home in heaven,
Why waste my time with you?
You lie and say you'll inherit God's throne,
But your days in the kingdom are through!

So talk your talk, but not to me;
May your words fall down in the dust.
It's God's word that has meaning for me in my life
It's in God where I'll put my trust.

"... I'm so tired, but hope is on the way. ..."

NECESSARY REST

Occasional weariness is just part of being human.

Acts 2:26-28

*...my flesh shall rest in hope: Because thou wilt not
leave my soul in hell, neither wilt thou suffer thine Holy One to see corruption.
Thou hast made known to me the ways of life; thou shalt make me full of joy with thy countenance.
(KJV)*

We cannot go non-stop without needing rest.

We can't forever look for our better selves without standing down for a short time to re-energize.

But because we rest our bodies, this doesn't mean that we are taking a rest from God.

When we rest, we should get off our feet, lean on something, relax in bed or a comfortable chair, take a hot bath. Do something that causes us to be still in order to pray, meditate, listen to God.

God designed us to work and to rest, and to have hope doing both.

Our hope should always stand tall.

"... I'm working on reformation and reconciliation so I can glorify God with all that I have. ..."

2 Corinthians 5:16-21

*From this time on we do not
think of anyone
as the world does.
In the past we thought of
Christ as the world thinks,
but we no longer
think of him in that way.
If anyone belongs to Christ,
there is a new creation.
The old things have gone;
everything is made new!
All this is from God.
Through Christ,
God made peace between
us and himself,
and God gave us the work
of telling everyone about the
peace we can have with him.
God was in Christ, making
peace between the
world and himself.
In Christ, God did not hold
the world guilty of it's sins.
And he gave us this message
of peace. So we have been
sent to speak for Christ.
It is as if God is calling to
you through us.
We speak for Christ when we
beg you to be at peace with
God.
Christ had no sin, but God
made him become sin so that
in Christ
we could become right with
God.
(NCV)*

WORK ON IT

Our spirituality requires
that we constantly work--
work on learning what
we have to change,
work on knowing what
we need to come to
terms with in our lives,
work on using our gifts
to give God glory,
work on spreading His word,
work on maintaining
a prayer life,
work on our worship ritual
and continual praise.

It is by spending time
on these things
that we glorify God.
It is important for us to
have harmony in our lives.

Only by being our best
can we give our best
to and for God.
Work on deserving
His grace.

Sometimes the work is hard,
sometimes it's a simple matter.
But it is an ongoing process,
because glorifying God
is an ongoing process.

After all, God is an ongoing
presence in our lives.

"... I'm struggling with knowing what's on my to-do list and actually revving myself up to get it accomplished. So I just keep telling myself, 'You can do this.' Between that thought and the body is the temple of God. ..."

OH YES I CAN, AND SO CAN YOU!

Judges 6:15-16

*"But LORD",
Gideon replied,
"I am the least
in my entire family."
The LORD said to him,
"I will be with you."
(NLT)*

Ephesians 3:20

*Now glory be to God
who by his mighty
power at work
within us is able
to do far more
than we would ever
dare to ask or even
dream of--infinitely
beyond our highest
prayers, desires,
thoughts, or hopes.
(TLB)*

I sat down one day to write a list
of all I wanted to be,
of all the things I had planned to do
to produce the best from me.

When I finished my list I was so surprised
at just how long it was.
So I told myself as I erased most of it,
*"I'm not able,
I can't
because...
I can't because I'm not smart;
I can't because it's too much;
I can't because I'm not tall;
I can't because I'm afraid;
I can't because I'm not rich;
I can't because I'm sure it's too hard;
I can't because I'm convinced they won't like it;
I can't because I'm convinced they won't like me."*

Then Jesus appeared and said to me,
"You can, because
I AM."

So,
if you think **you** can't,
and won't give God a try;
Then you don't deserve an answer to
"I wonder why?"

But if you lay your thoughts, your desires, your wishes
at the door to His temple, O what blessings He affixes!

"... I give God at least 15 to 30 minutes of my first hour each day and then I get into my work. It seems to make things go a lot better - its quiet and I feel so relaxed. ..."

Genesis 28:16

And Jacob awaked out of his sleep, and he said,
Surely the LORD is in this place; ...
(KJV)

Exodus 16:7

And in the morning,
then ye shall see the glory of the LORD; ...
(KJV)

1 Samuel 1:19

And they rose up in the morning early,
and worshipped before the LORD, ...
(KJV)

Psalms 5:3

Each morning I will look to you in heaven
and lay my requests before you,
praying earnestly.
(TLB)

Mark 1:35

And in the morning, rising up a great while before day,
he went out, and departed into a solitary place,
and there prayed.
(KJV)

FIRST THINGS FIRST

ALARM CLOCK JARRING ME AWAKE

THOUGHTS RACING FRANTICALLY

TODAY'S BUSY SCHEDULE ON MY MIND

CAR HORNS BLOWING OUTSIDE

FAMILY WAITING FOR BREAKFAST

WARNING OF POSSIBLE TERRORIST ATTACKS

TRASH TRUCK LIFTING THE DUMPSTERS

STILL TIRED FROM BEING UP LATE

RAIN IS GOING TO AFFECT TRAFFIC

GAS BILL HAS TO BE PAID TODAY

DIDN'T MEET TODAY'S DEADLINE

DOG NEXT DOOR BARKED ALL NIGHT

TV NEWS REPORTING ON THE WAR

FORGOT TO TURN ON DRYER LAST NIGHT

NEIGHBOR'S CHILD VERY ILL

The start of each new day

that we are given is cause

to spend a little quiet time with God.

After all, this day is a gift from Him,

and if we Thank Him

for the new day

that He has blessed us with,

it puts order in our steps

for the rest of the day.

Let Him know how grateful

you are for having

kept you through the night.

Tell Him that you're going to

use this new day to glorify Him,

to walk righteous in His word.

Then in the quiet stillness, listen.

Dear blessed heavenly Father, thank you for bringing me through the night and into this brand new day. I know, LORD that you have provided me with yet another opportunity to make a difference in this earthly kingdom, so that others may be more aware of your heavenly kingdom. Fill me with the Holy Spirit and let your light shine through me. Help me to avoid being intolerant. Help me to be more loving and compassionate today. I pray LORD for your gift of peace. Let me not suffer in fear. Help me to remember to keep my mind stayed on you, for you shall always be my refuge. I pray that those who are alone right now, Father, will be made aware of your presence in their lives and be strengthened. Let them know without a doubt that you are their constant companion. For those who are sad today, God, touch them with your joy, a joy that can only be found through you. For those who are dealing with illness, either in themselves, or the illness of their loved ones, help them know that you will sustain them. LORD, help me recognize and be of assistance today to someone in need. Be my guide and inspiration in all that I do today. These things I pray in the precious name of Jesus Christ our Savior. *Amen.*

"... I'm so very, VERY glad I know the worth and power of prayer. ..."

Psalms 42:8

*Day by day the LORD
also pours out his
steadfast love upon me,
and through the night I
sing his songs and pray
to God who gives me
life...
(TLB)*

Jeremiah 32:17

*Ah, LORD God!
Behold, You have made
the heavens and the
earth by Your great
power and outstretched
arm. There is nothing
too hard for You.
(NKJV)*

Psalms 147:5

*How great is our
LORD! His power is
absolute!
His understanding is
beyond
comprehension!
(NLT)*

PRAYER POWER

Prayer has an immeasurable value.
There can be no price put on it,
and there is nothing
that is strong enough
to negate it.
It is a force so strong
that nothing can overcome it.
It brings results.
Prayer is the armor that you need
to keep Satan out of your way.
It's how you worship,
praise and thank God.
It is your faith
pouring out
from your heart.
It's how you become
your most humble self,
telling God what
He already knows.
It is your responsibility to pray...
it is your privilege to pray.
Pray for others, for yourself,
for His continued blessings,
for your continued walk
in His path.

"... But I know we have to come down off the mountain to serve. ..."

MOUNTAINTOPS AND VALLEYS

Matthew 8:1-2

*When he was come
down from the
mountain,
great multitudes
followed him.
And, behold,
there came a leper
and worshiped him,
saying,
LORD, if thou wilt
thou canst make
me clean.
And Jesus put
forth his hand,
and touched him,
saying, I will;
be thou clean.
And immediately
his leprosy was
cleansed.
(KJV)*

Your mountaintop is wherever you go
to praise God and to thank Him
for your blessings.

It feels good being there,
basking in the glow of His warmth.

But what God gives you, He wants you to share.
So you have to come down off the mountain
to serve others.

Your assignment comes on the mountaintop,
but your tasks begin in the valley.

You don't lose that glow by coming
off the mountain.
You're soaking up even more of
God's warmth
when you share with others.

So take the flame of your mountaintop experiences
to the valleys and ignite the fire of Jesus in others.

"... I recognize what I cannot do. But I do pray and think about ways to help as a good team player. ..."

YOU CAN ALWAYS HELP

Mark 9:22-24

*...if you can do
anything for him,
please have pity
on us and help us.
Jesus said to
the father, "you said,
'If you can!'
All things are possible
for the one
who believes."
Immediately the father
cried out, "I do
believe! Help me to
believe more!"
(NCV)*

You cannot be all things to all people.
When you go to God in prayer,
ask Him for discernment so that you
might know what you can do
in a given situation.

Ask Him for guidance so that when
you offer your services to others,
no matter what their needs,
no matter what their circumstances,
you do not do it in such a way
that it will belittle or shame.

Also ask God to help you to
know your limits so that your efforts
are not too little nor
your promises too grand.

"... I'll ask for forgiveness. ..."

THE POWER OF FORGIVENESS

2 Chronicles 7:14

If my people, which are called by my name, shall humble themselves, and pray, and seek my face, and turn from their wicked ways; then will I hear from heaven, and will forgive their sin, and will heal their land.
(KJV)

Acts 26:18

...to open their eyes so they may turn from darkness to light, and from the power of Satan to God. Then they will receive forgiveness for their sins and be given a place among God's people, who are set apart by faith in me.
(NLT)

I knew it was wrong when I did it,
I said things I knew I shouldn't say;
But the day had been very stressful,
I just wanted everything my way.
So I set about chiding and demeaning,
No care for any thoughts but mine;
The friend whom I hurt was bewildered
But too kind to say I had crossed the line.

Alone after I turned and departed,
I thought about the things I did shout;
I wondered why I said such horrible words
That can never be pulled back once they're out.
I shouldn't blame the stress I was under,
I certainly can't blame the friend I hurt.
I only blame myself for stepping away from Christ
To wallow with Satan in his dirt.

I'm ashamed that I let him take over,
Embarrassed that I succumbed to his power;
God's word has been sown in my heart for so long,
How could I have given the enemy this hour?
With strength and my faith I did banish him,
Turned from Satan's darkness unto God's light;
In deep prayer I asked Christ's forgiveness,
Humbled myself to my friend, made things right.

My eyes are now open, no more darkness,
I've crushed the Wicked one under my heel;
In the light I asked for forgiveness,
My friend proved our friendship is real.
Dear Father God, thank you for mercy,
For your blessings each and every one.
I'll surrender my will to yours dear LORD
Until my days on this earth are done.

"... shouting and having a good time. ..."

Psalms 95:1

*Come, let us sing
to the LORD!
Let us give a joyous shout to
the rock of our salvation!
(NLT)*

Psalms 98:4-9

*Shout to the LORD,
all the earth;
break out in praise
and sing for joy!
Sing your praise to the
LORD with the harp,
with the harp and
melodious song,
with trumpets and the
sound of the ram's horn.
Make a joyful symphony
before the LORD, the King!
Let the sea and everything in
it shout his praise!
Let the earth and all living
things join in.
Let the rivers clap their
hands in glee!
Let the hills sing out their
songs of joy
before the LORD.
(NLT)*

HAVE A PRAISE PARTY
(SING WITH JOY, Y'ALL!)

Come and raise your arms,
  lift your hands to the sky;
If anyone questions you
  and dares to ask why,
Spin yourself around,
  leap and dance about,
Tell 'em you're praising the LORD
  with a joyful shout!

You won't need to call a caterer,
  no need to decorate;
Sing praises, have a good time
  and just celebrate!
Invite your family, your neighbors
  or party alone;
Shout so the angels up in heaven
  know you're one of God's own.

A rocking Holy Ghost party
  costs you nothing to throw;
Tell everyone you're praising God,
  someone they all should know!
There will be many happy faces,
  love-laughter-joy all around;
Hand-clapping, foot-stomping music
  to bless the heaven bound!

"... I'm still waiting to see if he shows me something different. ..."

GOD WILL LET YOU KNOW

Psalms 62:1

*Truly my soul waiteth upon God: from hi cometh my salvation.
(KJV)*

Just because God puts you in one place, it doesn't mean that He will keep you in that place. When His purpose has been served, He will show you a different path.

When you've prayed on a situation and made a decision, keep checking back with God to see if He wants you to make an adjustment.

Isaiah 40:31

*But they that wait upon the LORD shall renew their strength; they shall mount up with wings as eagles; they shall run, and not be weary; and they shall walk, and not faint.
(KJV)*

You may not always be where others want you to be but if you've given your life to God and He has guided you to a certain place, then that's where He wants you to be.

It may be a particular job, or a church, or even a particular state of mind. Just hold your place, ask Him what he wants for you and you will certainly get your answer.

"... I even sang, 'show me the way, LORD. I'm down here and I need your power, show me the way'. ..."

SEND THE LORD YOUR HEART-SONG

Ezra 3:11

*And they sang together
by course in praising
and giving thanks unto
the LORD; because he
is good, for his mercy
endureth for ever
(KJV)*

Revelation 15:3

*...and they were
singing the song of
Moses,
the servant of God,
and the song of the
Lamb:
"Great and
marvelous are
your doings,
LORD God
Almighty..."
(TLB)*

Singing a song in the LORD's Holy name
is a wonderful way to praise Him.
Singing to the LORD is a special way
of letting Him know how you feel.
Sending a song to the LORD fills your soul.

Whether it's a solemn song of pleading,
a contemporary foot-stomping hymn,
or perhaps an old-time gospel pearl,
just lifting your voice in refrain
to sing in His name is praising Him.

Sing to let the LORD know that you need help.
Sing and thank Him for every blessing.
Sing to Him to soothe your wounded spirit.
Sing to Him to calm your frightened soul.
Sing praises to Him to show your gratefulness.

Let your heart fill with songs of majesty.
Whether your voice matches heavenly choirs
or has no semblance of melody at all,
The tone that reaches the Savior's keen ear
will be as pure as the songs of angels.

If you ask for the LORD's blessings through prayer
or speak of your pain through song,
the LORD will show you the way to His side.
With His love and His power He will guide you,
while you're down here in such need of Him.

"... You know Toni, in order to receive more blessings, we must endure our afflictions, go through the valleys. But just pick up your cross, regardless of how heavy it seems to be...how hard it is to bear. Remember, you always have God with you. ..."

ENDURE

I sobbed the pain sorely, thinking no one was there,
Suddenly the breeze of His fingers gently swept through my hair.
I turned and looked around me, not one person did I see,
But a touch on my shoulder sent heavenly warmth through me.

I cried out in anguish, "Where are they, God, and where are you?
Only you know the why, LORD, tell me what did I do?"
I knelt and looked skyward, felt His hands cup my face;
Listened as He soothed me, wept in His embrace.

Knowing He was beside me, I asked Him to make me strong,
This pain from my loss had been with me for so long.
With both arms around me, He held me to His chest,
Whispered, "Some left you, some stayed, but I love you best."

With words just for me, such blessings He did impart;
He assured me that He knew of the ache in my heart.
He said part of my loss was purely His plan,
But some of it had to do with the free will He gave man.

He told me I could not fix it now, and neither would He,
Some things that happen are simply meant to be.
He said I should pray from the deepest part of my soul,
To trust and be faithful, knowing He is in control.

I asked Him to forgive me for burying myself in grief,
I thanked Him for His goodness, for bringing me relief.
He said, "It is not over yet, you're still in its hour,
But I promise you the sun's joy
once I lead you through this shower."

Luke 15:11,20

"A [wo]man had two sons. ...While the son was still a long way off, his [mo]ther saw him ... So the [mo]ther ran to him and hugged and kissed him.
(NCV)

"... If the LORD wants me there, he'll show me. ..."

ALL MAPPED OUT

Exodus 13:21

And the LORD went before them by day in a pillar of a cloud, to lead them the way; and by night in a pillar of fire, to give them light; to go by day and night: (KJV)

The LORD will always show you exactly where He wants you to be.

You need not ever feel lost, or wonder about the journey because He will guide you day and night.

So praise Him for the paths He has laid out for you and walked with you.

Thank Him for being that constant guide in your life.

And then, follow Him!

"... What God has for me, it is for me. ..."

MINE...ALL MINE

God is not the creator of
"one blessing fits all".

Matthew 6:8

*Be not ye therefore
like unto them:
for your Father
knoweth what things
ye have need of,
before ye ask him.
(KJV)*

God knows each one of us
and has specific blessings
for every one of us.

He will not give you
your neighbor's blessing
and your neighbor will not
get your blessing.

You are special in His sight,
unlike anyone else
He has ever made.

What He has for someone else
is not going to work for you.

God knows what you need,
when to give it to you and
how you are to use it
for His glory.

"... The offer sounded very good, but after a lot of prayer I am convinced that I do not need to part from the path that I am presently on. ..."

FOLLOWING GOD'S ROAD MAP

Hebrews 12:1-2

*...let us run with
endurance
the race that
God has set
before us.
We do this
by keeping
our eyes on
Jesus,
on whom our
faith
depends from
start to finish.
(KJV)*

In each person's life the paths are many
But the one God provides is better than any.

I chose some that were crooked and bumpy
With dangers around that made me quite jumpy.

The one mapped by God is straight and bright
With sure-footed paving, brightened by His light.

He entwines the paths so we encounter others
He wants us to treat all as sisters and brothers.

Along life's path there is much to see
But not all of those things are meant for me.

Although I may venture, sometimes go astray
God welcomes me back, guides me the right way.

I praise God's path with all my heart
Convicted by His love, I shall not depart.

"... I know in my heart that Satan has used all this other stuff; has tried to make me yield and distract me with his noise and foolishness. ..."

CAN YOU HEAR ME NOW?

The time comes when you have to show the LORD that you are listening.

Psalms 107:29-30

*He calms
the storm,
so that
it's waves are
still.
Then they
are glad
because
they are
quiet;
so he guides them
to their desired
haven.
(NKJV)*

No matter what distractions surround you, God is always whispering in your ear, giving you guidance, divulging secrets for your heart alone, revealing destinations that He has chosen for you, imparting directions to the paths paved for your life.

He could stop those distractions around you, quiet the noises, just as He calmed the sea. But He wants you to be able to discern His voice in the midst of any storm. He leaves it up to you to quiet those storms in your life that tend to keep you from hearing His voice.

No matter what else is going on, only God's voice is the one that will matter. Listen for His voice, yield only to Him, be distracted only in obedience to Him.

Give Him your time, give Him your attention, and your thoughts. Succumb only to His voice.

"... Unless the LORD comes a different way, I'm going to stay the course until He makes it so clear. ..."

GOING THE RIGHT WAY

Exodus 14:13

And Moses said unto the people, "Do not be afraid.
Stand still, and see the salvation of the LORD, which he will accomplish for you.
(NKJV)

Romans 8:28

And we know that all things work together for good to them that love God, to them who are the called according to his purpose.
(KJV)

God put me on this path
and on His path I will stay,
Sometimes I don't quite understand
why He led me this way.
I do not feel afraid of what
He has in store for me,
I only want to do His will
knowing what will be will be.
I'll ever praise the LORD,
wait while He makes it clear
What I am to do for Him
and my purpose for being here.
Though others may not understand,
may tell me I must stop,
I will follow God and keep the pace
to reach His mountaintop.
I'll stay the course that He has set
in spite of what befalls me
I promised the LORD to live for Him
until the day He calls me.

"... There is hope and I know it. ..."

Romans 15:13   ## *HOPE*

*God
who gives
you hope
will keep
you happy
and full
of peace
as you
believe
in him.
I pray that
God will
help you
overflow
with hope
in him
through the
Holy Spirit's
power
within you.
(TLB)*

There is hope
Here in my spirit,
Ever moving in my soul.
Resurrecting dreams once buried
Each one now becoming whole.

Inspired by hope and blessed by Your grace,
Savior, my faith keeps my hope in place.

Hope and prayer refresh my spirit,
Open the door to brighter days.
Promises spoken and promises kept.
Evidence of God's will and ways...

...and I know it!

"... Hallelujah, Praise the LORD, O Give Thanks unto God, for his mercy endureth forever. I am just so overjoyed by God's continued abundant blessings. He just keeps on giving more and more ..."

Psalms 40:5

Many, O LORD my God, are Your wonderful works which You have done; and Your thoughts which are toward us cannot be recounted to You in order; If I would declare and speak of them, They are more than can be numbered.
(NKJV)

MORE AND MORE

More than I could ever want
More than I could ever need
More than I could ever get
The LORD
        blesses me
                    indeed!

More than I ever dare to expect
More than I ever hope to repay
More than I ever thought to deserve
The LORD
        blesses in a
                    mighty way!

"... God gave me traveling mercies - hallelujah. ..."

TRAVELING MERCIES

I'm on the road nearly every day
I don't start a trip until I pray
Don't leave the house until I say
"God give me traveling mercies."

Luke 13:22

Along the streets are children at play
Pedestrians who need the right of way
Sometimes bad weather, foggy and gray
"God give me traveling mercies."

*And he went
through the cities
and villages,
teaching, and
journeying toward
Jerusalem.
(KJV)*

Over bridges and highways, and across the bay
Through traffic that causes a major delay
On smoothed paved streets and back roads of clay
"God give me traveling mercies."

Through the windshield shines the sun's bright ray
Right over my hood flies a springtime blue jay
I move along as gently as I may,
"God give me traveling mercies."

Each evening when in my bed I lay
And recall that everything went okay
I look to God and again I pray,
"Hallelujah!"

"... God is with me, and always has been with me. He has brought me such a mighty long way and for that I say thank you Jesus. ..."

John 14:16

*And I will pray the Father
and he shall give you another Comforter,
that he may abide with you for ever;
(KJV)*

Deuteronomy 5:33

*Live the way the LORD your God
has commanded you
so that you may live
and have what is good ...
(NCV)*

Genesis 9:9

*And I, behold, I establish my covenant
with you, and with your seed after you;
(KJV)*

Matthew 28:20

*Teaching them to observe all things
whatsoever I have commanded you:
and, lo, I am with you alway,
even unto the end of the world. Amen.
(KJV)*

THANK YOU JESUS

We can never thank Jesus enough. Wherever we are in our lives, God is with us, was with us from the beginning and will continue to be with us. Anyone who has that kind of staying power needs to be thanked continuously, and it still wouldn't be enough.

God is
with me
     Thank you Jesus

Has been
with me
     Thank you Jesus

He has
brought me
     Thank you Jesus

Such a
long way
     Thank you Jesus

And for
that I
     Thank you Jesus

Praise, shout,
and say
     Thank you Jesus

Thank you
Jesus
     Thank you Jesus.

"... Don't try to figure it out. If you believe its God's will, play it out and just see what the outcome would be. ..."

DO YOU FEEL LIKE JOB?

Job 42:12

*So the LORD
blessed the
latter end
of Job
more than his
beginning.
(KJV)*

We never know for sure why certain situations in our lives happen or how they will turn out. For many of us, no matter how dedicated we are to God, the question "Why?" rests at least momentarily in our minds even if it never crosses our lips.

God knows that we will sometimes wonder why certain things have come upon us. It is only human. But if we are faithful, we will not dwell on it. Much of what He knows is a mystery to us, and beyond our understanding.

Even Job, a person who was blameless, upright and fiercely committed to God, yelled at God -- a little bit.

So we must pray while always believing that God can do everything. When He is pointing you in a direction that is unclear, where your burdens seem unduly heavy, when your life is in turmoil, don't give up. Praise God for the test. As hard as it may be, thank Him for choosing you for this storm...for choosing this storm for you. Praise Him for this learning experience, for this moment of doubt and uncertainty, because your blessing will result in a new ministry of reassurance which God will fit into the plan He has for you.

And if you, like Job, should happen to yell at God -- a little bit -- He will understand and forgive you.

"... on the right path to moving forward and really forgetting about the unpleasant things that are behind me. ..."

LOOK FORWARD

Not every path we follow is smooth.
Sometimes we trip, stumble, even fall.
But with faith and God's help we can manage
to pick ourselves up and continue on
our journey.

Genesis 19:26

*But his wife
looked back
from behind him,
and she became
a pillar of salt.
(KJV)*

Once we're up and moving again, it serves no
purpose to look back at the pebble that caused
our fall.

We need to be grateful for having been able to get
beyond that. We need to keep looking forward,
eyes focused on the prize God has in store
for us.

Just as God forgives our sins, our past, our fallen
moments, we too need to leave those things in
the past.

If we continue to look back we're slowing our
journey, not seeing what God has put ahead of us,
and may possibly miss the blessings that He has in
store for us.

"... The LORD has been dealing with me. ..."

Psalms 139:1-5

O LORD, you have examined my heart and know everything about me. You know when I sit down or stand up. You know my every thought when far away. You chart the path ahead of me and tell me where to stop and rest. Every moment you know where I am. You know what I am going to say even before I say it, LORD. You both precede and follow me. You place your hand of blessing on my head.
(NLT)

WHICH WAY?

The LORD continually monitors your walk.

If you take the way that leads away from Him, He will always let you know that there is a better way.

God is full of kindness and He will work with you through any crisis.

He will not leave you all alone, even when you are straying away from Him.

If things are chaotic in your life, meditate. Praise His name and offer thanks for His goodness.

Ask Him for His guidance and then listen.

"... GOD has brought us through and over. ..."

Isaiah 43:2-3

When thou passest through the waters, I will be with thee; and through the rivers, they shall not overflow thee: when thou walkest through the fire, thou shalt not be burned; neither shall the flame kindle upon thee.
For I am the LORD thy God, the Holy One of Israel, thy Savior...
(KJV)

GOD IS WITH US

Through water or fire or dark of night
God is in our presence;
His goodness, His grace, His holy light
God is always with us

He walks with us through the best of times
Carries us through the worst,
Stands with us when we need to be still,
For that we must keep Him first.

"... Let us bow down unto Him and say thank you. ..."

Ephesians 3:14

For this cause I bow my knees unto the
Father of our LORD Jesus Christ,...
(KJV)

Philippians 2:10

That at the name of Jesus
every knee should bow
of things in heaven,
and things in earth,
and things under the earth;...
(KJV)

Psalms 95:6

O come, let us worship and bow down:
let us kneel before the LORD our maker.
(KJV)

Romans 14:11

For the Scriptures say,
" 'As surely as I live,' says the LORD,
'every knee will bow to me
and every tongue will confess
allegiance to God.'
(NLT)

BOW AND WORSHIP

I drove

out to the country one day for a peaceful farmland ride.

I saw

a farmer in his fields of hay, so I pulled off to the side.

I said

"When I was up on the hill in my car, I thought I saw clumps of hay."

He said

"You saw the people here just kneeling down to pray."

I said

"But look at this soaking ground, it's wet and covered in mud."

He said

"It doesn't matter where you kneel to give thanks for Jesus' blood."

I asked

"But they're so poor; why dirty their only clothes down in that mess?"

He told me

"God gave them this farm, their lives are immeasurably blessed."

I asked

"Why can't they thank Him while they are standing up?"

He said

"Because His many blessings overflows in each one's cup."

I asked,

"If they've accomplished so much why can't they stand tall?"

He said,

"Without Christ the LORD they would have none of this at all."

I said,

as on my knees I fell, "Thank you Father for this day."

He said

"My child I will bless you as you bow down to pray."

"... I enter into God's presence. ..."

HIS AWESOME PRESENCE

Be still
and feel yourself being transported
            to the throne of the King,
Feel your spirit move
between heaven and earth...
            ...thank Him for everything.

Be quiet
and listen for His voice welcoming you
            into His presence,
Let Him whisper to you
His plan for your life...
            ...His gift of your very essence.

Exodus 33:14

And he said,
My presence
shall go with thee,
and I will give
thee rest.

Be humble
and acknowledge that you could never
            be worthy enough.
He gives grace you don't deserve,
loves you always...
            ...Keeps you when times are tough.

Be obedient
and He will make His glorious presence
            known to you,
Hold on to your faith and
seek to know Him better...
            ...He'll be with you in all you go through.

"... I feel like shouting cause I came out of that wilderness. ..."

Exodus 13:18, 21-22

God led the people about, through the way of the wilderness...
And the LORD went before them by day in a pillar of a cloud, to lead them the way; and by night in a pillar of fire, to give them light; to go by day and night:
He took not away the pillar of the cloud by day, nor the pillar of fire by night, from before the people
(KJV)

OUT OF THE WILDERNESS

There's not a more joyous moment than when God brings you through a situation and you KNOW that it was God who brought you out.

You can't help but shout. Just stop and think, when you were lost and felt you were wandering aimlessly, did you know and acknowledge God's presence with you in the wilderness?

"... I've been praying and that has really been a blessing. ..."

Matthew 6:9-15

*After this manner
therefore pray ye:
Our Father which art
in heaven, Hallowed
be thy name.
Thy kingdom come.
Thy will be done in earth,
as it is in heaven.
Give us this day
our daily bread.
And forgive us our debts
as we forgive our debtors.
And lead us not into
temptation, but deliver us
from evil: For thine is the
kingdom, and the power, and
the glory, for ever. Amen.
For if ye forgive men their
trespasses, your heavenly
Father will also forgive you:
But if ye forgive not men their
trespasses, neither will your
Father forgive your
trespasses.
(KJV)*

KNOW PRAYER

Our Father
...I am your child on my knees
Hallowed
...my adoration can never match your majesty
Thy kingdom
...you've set aside a place just for me
Thy will
...you've laid out the plan for my life
Give us
...I ask for what is already mine
Forgive us
...you don't hold a grudge when I go astray
Deliver us
...your hand guides me to safety
Power and glory
...your omnipotence overwhelms me
Amen
...Amen and amen.

"... God sure enough knows what we need just as we need it. ..."

GOD KNOWS

Psalms 139:1-6

*O LORD, you have examined
my heart and know
everything about me. You
know when I sit down or
stand up.
You know my every thought
when far away. You chart the
path ahead of me and tell me
where to stop and rest.
Every moment you know
where I am. You know what I
am going to say even before I
say it, LORD.
You both precede and follow
me. You place your hand of
blessing on my head.
Such knowledge is too
wonderful for me,
too great for me to know!
(NLT)*

God planned us,
designed us,
knew all about us
before we were ever conceived.

He hears us,
and loves us
pours blessings upon us
because in our faith He believed.

He guards us
Stands by us
Puts his armor upon us,
So by Satan we won't be deceived.

God knows us,
Gives to us,
Issues His holy word for us,
So by faith His grace will be received.

"... Keep the prayers going up. ..."

"PRAYER-TIME" TIME

Acts 6:4

*But we will give
ourselves continually to
prayer,
and to the ministry of the
word.
(KJV)*

Do you have a certain time each day to pray? Perhaps you have scheduled a few minutes each morning to pray. Or maybe it's on your appointment calendar to pray each night before bedtime after you've brushed your teeth and put on your pajamas.

But what about when you're walking down the steps with a load of laundry. Do you pray then? Or how about when you're looking for the remote to change the channel on the television. Is there a prayer on your lips then? Watching your car going through the car wash....what's the prayer for that moment? What exactly is the right moment to pray to God when you are changing the blade on your lawnmower?

A prayer is not a "schedule" event. It's a word to God at any time, during any task or event, accepted by God at any time, during any sorrow or joy.

Always pray. Any time.

"... I want my will to be lost in His. ..."

LET'S HAVE
CATERPILLAR WILL

Psalms 143:10

Teach me to do thy will;
for thou art my God:
thy spirit is good;
lead me into the land
of uprightness.
(KJV)

Matthew 26:42

"O My Father,
if this cup cannot
pass away from Me
unless I drink it,
Your will be done."
(NKJV)

Often we want so much out of life that we don't stop to consider if what we are going after is what God has willed for our lives.

So we make hasty decisions, incorrect assumptions, missteps. Not until we see the disastrous results of our willfulness, do we realize that we were following our will instead of His.

When you praise God, when you meditate on His grace, ask Him to give you the will of a caterpillar. The caterpillar moves through life for a while as it was designed to do until one day it becomes enwrapped in a cocoon and is provided additional growth. Eventually, after a certain period of time, it emerges as a beautiful butterfly.

If we allow ourselves to be wrapped in the cocoon of God's will, we will experience a glorious growth that puts us more in tune with His plan for us. If we don't rush it, just believe and let life take its natural course, our change will come. Then just think how beautiful our countenance will be when we emerge.

"... I was convicted by Ephesians 4:29 and I'm going to squash flesh and develop some more fruit; the enemy wants me bad but he can't get me. ..."

CONVICTED

Ephesians 4:29

Let no corrupt communication proceed out of your mouth, but that which is good to the use of edifying, that it may minister grace unto the hearers. (KJV)

Sometimes our own will, our flesh,
our "humanness," tells us
to avenge someone who has
done us wrong,
to walk a path that God
has not directed,
to behave in a manner
that might be
hurtful to someone.

But we must remember
That our Father
has provided us with
fruit to enhance our spirit,
fruit to give us patience,
fruit to win souls
and not destroy them,
fruit to enable us to be more
Christ-like.

"... I'm just waiting to see how God works this out for His glory and I can witness - what folks meant for bad, God meant it for good. ..."

GOD WILL WORK IT OUT

God works out our problems
to His satisfaction.

Acts 5:38-39

And now I say to you,
keep away from these men
and let them alone;
for if this plan
or this work is of men,
it will come to nothing;
but if it is of God,
you cannot overthrow it
lest you even be found
to fight against God.

Sometimes there is not a thing
we can do but go to Him
and trust Him to be with us
and to bring us safely out
on the other side of that problem.

We cannot always stop others from
mistreating us. But we can know
that God will take care of us
in the way He deems necessary.

When we are surrounded by bad times,
unfortunate circumstances,
impossible situations,
we need to just wait on God
and let Him make a way.

We must continue to praise Him
for all His goodness.
Meditate, talk to Him
to let Him know how we feel,
how we are affected
by what is going on.

Then we must thank Him
for all of our blessings,
for all of His grace.

"... The very BEST of best friends is Jesus. He is so good to me. He supplies all my needs and has given me, so many times, the desires of my heart. ..."

A FRIEND WHO KNOWS

Exodus 33:11

*And the LORD spake unto Moses face to face, as a man speaketh unto his friend.
(KJV)*

Proverbs 22:11

*Whoever loves pure thoughts and kind words will have even the king as a friend
(NCV)*

John 15:15

*Henceforth I call you not servants; for the servant knoweth not what his LORD doeth: but I have called you friends; for all things that I have heard of my Father I have made known unto you.
(KJV)*

John 15:16

*You did not choose me; I chose you.
(NCV)*

There is no friend like Jesus.

No matter how many
earthly friends you have,
all of them together
could not provide you with
all that Jesus gives you.

They could never know
you the way Jesus does.

They had to wait until you
were born to know you.

They could never
know your every need
the way Jesus does.

They have to wait
until you make a request
to know your needs.

Praise Him for giving
you what you need.

Meditate on His generosity.

Give thanks
not because He gives
you what you ask for,
but because He gives you
life, love and joy.

"... Nobody can do me like Jesus can. How many folks would be willing to die for you; how many folks are willing to love you, sight unseen in the flesh. ..."

JESUS, OUR OWN

Matthew 28:20

*And be sure of this:
I am with you
always,
even to the end
of the age.
(NLT)*

How wonderful it is to know that Jesus' only concern
is us.
It probably is also somewhat selfish on our part
to think that someone exists only for us...
to meet our every need,
to love us unconditionally,
to do all of this not because of
anything we have done,
but simply because we are here.

To become human like us in order to experience
what we live every day.
To become human like us in order to show us how to
live like Him every day.

John 15:13

*Greater love
hath no man
than this,
that a man
lay down his life
for his friends.
(KJV)*

To give up His life because He wants us not to
hurt, suffer or feel pain.
To give up His life in a manner that caused Him to
hurt, suffer and feel pain.

He exists to love us,
exists to watch over us,
to be with us during the worst times of our lives
...and the best.

To plead a case before His Father
on our behalf.
To hold our hand and guide us
to His Father's throne.

"... I spent the morning thanking God for his son Jesus, who suffered and bled and died for our sins. ..."

John 3:16

For God so loved the world, that he gave his only begotten Son...
(KJV)

Romans 8:32

Since he did not spare even his own Son for us but gave him up for us all, won't he also surely give us everything else?
(TLB)

Psalms 22:1

My God, my God! Why have you forsaken me?
Why do you remain so distant?
Why do you ignore my cries for help?
(NLT)

Matthew 27:46

Jesus called out with a loud voice, "Eli, Eli, lema sabachthani?"
which means, "My God, my God, why have you forsaken me?"
(TLB)

Romans 5:6-9

When we were utterly helpless with no way of escape, Christ came at just the right time and died for us sinners who had no use for him. Even if we were good, we really wouldn't expect anyone to die for us, though, of course, that might be barely possible. But God showed his great love for us by sending Christ to die for us while we were still sinners. And since by his blood he did all this for us as sinners, how much more will he do for us now that he has declared us not guilty?
(NLT)

ARE YOU A GOOD PARENT?

Imagine this scenario -- you're sitting in a beautiful park, tall green trees, colorful flowers, birds, butterflies, families strolling through, couples holding hands, good friends chatting, children giggling, people sharing precious moments, beautiful blue sky -- the perfect day, a wonderful gift from God.

You hear squeals of laughter as your little boy comes running to you through the grass. His little arms wrap around your leg, you reach down and pick him up and the two of you joyfully make your way home.

Later on, you see the news reports on television and hear that there was a purse snatching in that park, a robbery in the bank on the corner, a murder across town, someone was badly beaten in an alley a few blocks away from your home. You think to yourself, "These are terrible things and something should be done to stop it."

What could be done to stop it? Could you do something if you thought it would make a difference? As a parent, how much of a sacrifice would you be willing to make to protect your children?

There was one parent who did do something about it. One parent who relinquished something so cherished, that it seems unimaginable to most of us. Could you have made the sacrifice He made? Could you allow your beautiful little son to die so that the criminals might turn their lives around? Could you see the thorns piercing his skin and let it happen? Can you imagine the nails driven through your precious son's hands and feet? Could you allow the flesh to be torn from his body and his wounds soaked in salt and vinegar in order to save your neighbors? Could you see blood streaming down his little cheeks in hopes that the cold-hearted would turn their lives over to God? If you had the power to change things and prevent this cruelty from happening, when *you* heard your son crying out to you, "Daddy, please...why?" could you let this brutality against him continue without interfering, all for the sake of community peace?

Praise God...you don't have to. Praise God...He gave His son so that yours would have everlasting life. Praise God...a stronger father, a better parent than any of us could ever be.

Praise God.

"... I was just sitting here thinking about how wonderful God is. He is so loving, so giving, He is so helpful and always right on time. I can't thank him enough for all he does. ..."

SO THANKFUL

Colossians 3:15, 17

...let the peace of God rule in your hearts, ...and be thankful. And whatever you do in word or deed, do all in the name of the LORD Jesus, giving thanks to God the Father through Him. (NKJV)

When I woke up yesterday morning
I felt the Savior's love.
I arose and began to thank Him,
To reach out to my Father above.

And as I went through my day
So many things happened to me;
I thanked Him over and over again
And some more last night on my knees.

But late in the night not satisfied
That I had thanked Him enough,
I whispered to Him, "Thank you Father;
Helping me this much must be tough."

Romans 5:5

*Then, when that happens,
we are able to hold our heads high no matter what happens and know that
all is well, for we know how dearly God loves us,
and we feel this warm love everywhere within us because God has given us the
Holy Spirit to fill our hearts with his love
(TLB)*

Softly He said, "You can't keep up,
Or match blessings one-by-one.
I have so much to give to you
Breaking even can never be done."

"Thank me in your daily prayers,
And then go about your day.
Live your life to glorify my name
Knowing I'm by your side to stay."

"Speak of me with those you meet;
Let your works be an affirmation.
Your love for me shines from your heart
I am thanked by your adoration."

When I settled back down to sleep,
God's spirit moved through my soul.
He let me know He was always there
Giving, loving, keeping me whole.

"... I thank God for his patience with me. ..."

PATIENCE

Romans 5:1-5

Therefore being justified by faith, we have peace with God through our LORD Jesus Christ: By whom also we have access by faith into this grace wherein we stand, and rejoice in hope of the glory of God. And not only so, but we glory in tribulations also: knowing that tribulation worketh patience; And patience, experience; and experience, hope: And hope maketh not ashamed; because the love of God is shed abroad in our hearts by the Holy Ghost which is given unto us.
(KJV)

How often have you found yourself saying, "I'm just fed up!" Or maybe you've thought to yourself, "I've taken all I can take of this situation." Perhaps you are waiting for something that seems to take too long to happen. How do you react during these times? Do you simply give up? Do you decide that you have given more than enough time and just cut off the waiting?

Do you think God ever feels that way about us? What if He put us on a schedule? What if when we made the decision to go to Him, He was no longer there for us? When we found time for Him, He no longer had time for us?

Knowing that God is always there for us...any time, whatever the hour, whatever the circumstances, no matter what the reason for our delay...can make us complacent sometimes. Make us take God for granted.

If you are not on the plane when it is scheduled to leave at four o'clock, it will leave the airport without you. Fortunately, God does not have a schedule. God can take flight, but would never leave without us. He gives us until our very last breath to come to Him.

He wears no watch, has no checklist, no calendar, no curfew, no downtime. We ought to always sing praises for that fact alone. He's patient. He's there. And although we should turn to Him sooner rather than later, when we finally decide "now is the time" God makes it His time too.

O, praise Him for his mercy...meditate on His goodness...be joyful for His patience.

"... My life is to glorify God; how better to do this but through trials and tribulations. ..."

THROUGH IT ALL

John 16:33

*These things
I have spoken to you,
that in Me
you may have peace.
In the world
you will have
tribulation;
but be of good cheer,
I have overcome
the world.
(NKJV)*

Made in His image, designed by His plan
My life is to glorify God.
Given the will to follow His path
With Him no day is too hard.

I know that life is not all smooth
I know that I may falter;
Through every step, though good or bad
I pray upon His altar.

Through every trial that I encounter
Through all my tribulations,
I look for God right by my side
and begin my celebration.

"... I am an over comer, and I am a child of the King, I will be fine. I love the LORD. ..."

PRAYER OF THANKS

John 12:36

While ye have light, believe in the light, that ye may be the children of light.
(KJV)

I come to you LORD, giving thanks to God the Father and you His son. I pray for the continuous grace and mercy that you have shown to me. Thank you for the guidance and protection that has been bestowed upon me. LORD you have always held my hand and sheltered me as a father should. For that and so much more, I love you and I thank you. Thank you dear LORD for the opportunity to discern your way from the world's way, your peace from the world's torment, your goodness from the world's harshness.

Father, I claim the resolution of this problem that has arisen in my life. I know that you solved it before it ever happened. I pray that I will soon find my way through this crisis so that I may learn from it and thereby be equipped to teach others. My Father, you have taught me well. I am eating your word and waiting patiently as it dissolves throughout my soul and strengthens me. I feel the Holy Spirit moving through me, filling me up, nourishing my own spirit.

I am aware of the growth of my character as I shed my old garments handed down to me from the world and put on the new garments patterned just for me by You my heavenly Father. I've learned so much through your word, with more still yet to learn.

I acknowledge that it is only by trusting in you that I am able to effectively bear whatever burdens come upon me. As your child, I will continue to rely upon your instruction. In the name of Jesus Christ, our LORD, I pray.

Amen.

"... I can't tell you how I feel, except stretched and know that God has my back, my sides and my front and all over me. ..."

THE PARABLE OF THE LITTLE RUBBER BAND

2 Corinthians 10:14

For we stretch not ourselves beyond our measure, as though we reached not unto you: for we are come as far as to you also in preaching the gospel of Christ. (KJV)

In the back of the drawer, behind the pencils and pens, between the ball of string and the box of air fresheners, next to the trash bag ties, under the expired coupons and twisted around one of the blades of the scissors, there was a little rubber band. It had been in that drawer for such a long, long time; ever since that day months ago when someone had taken it off the celery and dropped it in. After that whenever anything was put in the drawer, the rubber band got pushed farther and farther to the back, until no one even knew it was there any more. It had watched as brand new bags full of rubber bands were put in the drawer. And the little rubber band got ignored as those rubber bands in the bags were taken out one-by-one to be used, to stretch their arms around various things to hold them together. One day the little rubber band saw someone rummaging through the drawer and heard a voice saying, "Daddy, the pages are loose and falling out of my Bible. If I take it to Sunday school like this, I might lose some of the pages. But all of the rubber bands I see in this bag are too large." Her father said to her, "Please give me the scissors out of the drawer and I will open this new bag of rubber bands. Maybe we'll find a smaller one in here." When she pulled the scissors out of the drawer the little rubber band was still wrapped around the blade. The little girl saw the rubber band and told her father that she would use that one. He thought it might be too small. But they tried it anyway. The little rubber band was so excited about finally being out of the drawer that it put all of its effort into stretching, *stretching*, **stretching** wide enough to fit around the Bible. And it did. The little girl was so pleased that she wouldn't lose any of her pages now. Her father looked at the front, back and sides of the Bible to make sure the rubber band wasn't twisted, then told her, "That little rubber band stretched just enough to hold all of God's blessings."

*Sometimes when we are feeling stretched,
it may be that God is trying to make more room
for the blessings He has in store for us.*

"... We all should use the gifts God gave us and hone our talents and abilities for His glory. ..."

WHO ASKED?

Using the gift God gave you
You go about your task.
But tell me, my talented sisters,
When did you approach Him to ask?
When you take a look at your work
And think you've done your best,
Just tell me this, my brothers,
When did you make your request?
You create a beautiful painting
Thank God for the idea and the notion.

2 Timothy 1:6

*...fan into flames
the spiritual gifts
God gave you...
(NLT)*

Your lifesaving skills are second to none
And you thank Him for calming the ocean.
Your singing can be heard in concert halls.
You thank Him for that voice so pure.
You thank Him in the research lab
For helping you find a cure.
You thank Him for your talent to preach,
Your sermons make spirits soar.
You thank Him for strength in your legs and arms,
As an athlete you've won trophies galore.
But when did you ask for this talent of yours?
Do you think you've ever been without it?
Did God ever say, "List the things you might want,
Come back and we'll talk about it."
You never asked God to give you that gift,
Never had to petition what He gave you.
He didn't need a request or handwritten note
In order to send His son to save you.
He knew before time just who you would be,
Knew exactly what His world would need;
Planned a gift just for you to share with mankind,
Talent to honor Him in word and in deed.
So feel blessed and continue to thank Him;
Give praise, show appreciation
For the one-of-a-kind gift He designed only for you
At some point before your creation.

POEMS BY REQUEST

O ccasionally I am asked to write a poem, devotion or speech that addresses a certain need or event within my church. After assurances from the LORD that we can do this together, I use the theme of the event and the related scripture to find inspiration.

Sometimes the words flow easily as I sit in front of my computer; other times God chooses to require more effort on my part to find the exact spiritual tone required to honor the request. In every case, it is pure joy for me to contribute in whatever way I can.

The following poems are included:

- *"I'm Just Loving Me"* - A greeting card verse for a Women in Touch Ministry workshop

- *"...Of Roses and Doves"* - Theme poem for the premier issue of the Women's Ministry magazine

- *"Women of God: Willing to Live a Holy Lifestyle"* – 2003 Women's Day theme poem

- *"A More Excellent Retreat"* - Afterthoughts of the 2002 Fort Foote Baptist Church Women's Retreat

- *"Advent"* - Poem for a Christmas issue of our church newsletter

Even outside the context of the events indicated here, these poems serve as effective *"Praise and Meditation Starters."*

"... We want to give each of the women who attend the fellowship this Saturday a greeting card. The theme of the workshop is 'I'm Just Loving Myself.' The scripture reference is Matthew 22:37-40. Can you design the card and maybe create a verse for it? The discussion is going to revolve around how we go about loving ourselves when burdens have us bound. So whatever you can take from that. ..."

Matthew 22:37-40

Jesus replied, "You must love the LORD your God with all your heart, all your soul, and all your mind. This is the first and greatest commandment. A second is equally important: 'Love your neighbor as yourself.' All the other commandments and all the demands of the prophets are based on these two commandments."
(NLT)

I'M JUST LOVING ME

I'm taking a moment to honor myself
And that's the way it should be
'Cause I love God and my neighbor too
And I'm just loving me!

I praise myself in my private time
Marvel at my natural beauty
And maybe no one else agrees
But I'm just loving me!

My self-love is the cornerstone
Of the love I give abundantly
Established by the word of God
So I'm just loving me!

"... would you like to write a poem for the premier issue of our new magazine, 'Of Roses and Doves' ..."

...OF ROSES AND DOVES

We are blessed with this ministry of words and thoughts
of God-centered wisdom, and truth;
Our shared sister space where we write of His love,
With the faith and devotion of Ruth.
We will gather and pray for divine inspiration
...not to see if God is real;
But to spread His word, to soothe,
to teach our sisters...and to heal.

Let us whisper of beauty, of grace from above,
Let us whisper
...of roses and doves.

We daughters of the King share a family tree,
Nurtured by a wondrous ancestor;
No matter who we are He'll provide us with strength
To find our voice, as He did for Esther.
With lessons of His works we will tell of God's glory,
With praise and thanksgiving, His grace.
In gladness we'll reveal the dreams that we hold,
Bear witness of His power and embrace.

Let us whisper of beauty, of grace from above,
Let us whisper
...of roses and doves.

We will share with each other the joy that we know,
Write of the paths that we chose;
Plant encouraging thoughts in this garden of words,
Watch it bloom like a sweet, precious rose.
We will summon the yearnings from deep in our hearts,
Use our gifts to write of God's love;
Share testimony that makes a soul take flight,
As on the wings of a soaring dove.

Let us whisper of beauty, of grace from above,
Let us whisper
...of roses and doves.

Psalms 26:7

That I may publish with the voice of thanksgiving, and tell of all thy wondrous works.
(KJV)

"... At the Women's Day planning meeting last night someone suggested that we ask you to write a poem for the occasion. If you have the time and find that God puts something on your heart, would you mind doing this for us? The theme is 'Women of God: Willing to Live a Holy Lifestyle', and the scripture is 2 Timothy 1:9 ..."

2 Timothy 1:9

Who hath saved us, and called us with an holy calling,
not according to our works, but according to his own purpose and grace,
which was given us in Christ Jesus before the world began,...
(KJV)

WOMEN OF GOD: WILLING TO LIVE A HOLY LIFESTYLE

We are daughters of the deity, embracing the holiness of God
Following the footsteps of Lois and Eunice in a faithful promenade.
We were planned by Holy inspiration to receive God's transforming grace
Which He bestowed upon each of us before our names ever had a face.
Saved and called into existence, chosen by God, given a purpose of our own,
Through holy work we praise His name, with Jesus as our cornerstone.
In preparation for our eternal reward we strive to be like Christ--
Living in holiness, strong in our faith, our hope never sacrificed.

Through prayer we look to the Lamb of God for our strength in an unholy world,
Sidestepping the traps and evil tricks that Satan has often unfurled.
We may find that living the holy life is not always an easy task;
Help is not always in the form we expect from God, not exactly as we ask.
We must keep in mind He has promised us everything we need for life,
Trust the Holy Spirit for sanctification, know Christ is with us through strife.
God would never ask us to do the impossible, He knows what we can achieve,
It is up to us to live a holy lifestyle, do good works, love the LORD and believe.

We are blessed to have this God given power, this holiness, our Christian calling;
Standing before His marvelous light, our obedience will keep us from falling.
In this war against earthly yearnings and desires we must resist, not be enticed.
We must hold fast the pattern of faith and love which are in our Savior Jesus Christ.
We are blessed with every spiritual blessing and humbly submit to God's
perfect will,
Thankfully saved by Christ, living as holy women is His purpose we hope to fulfill.
Just as He loved us and chose us in Him, we will be holy before Him in love;
Holy, without fault in His eyes, without blame, seeking our perfect home above.

Having therefore these promises, beloved,
let us secure perfect holiness through the fear of God.

"... We want to put together a special issue of the magazine '...Of Roses and Doves' based on the Women's Retreat. Do you think you could come up with a poem for us? Just think about it and see where the LORD leads you. ..."

A MORE EXCELLENT RETREAT

1 Corinthians 12:31

...and yet shew I unto you a more excellent way. (KJV)

The parking lot full of family and friends,
three buses, luggage, laughter and lunch;
So many women prepared to follow God's path
On something much deeper than a hunch.
Gathered in anticipation for this weekend retreat
Thrilled faces of sisters with one purpose,
To find a more excellent way to honor the LORD,
To live the life He requires...strong and virtuous.
They prayed for traveling mercy, not just for the drive,
But for each woman's sacred trip to God's throne;
One hundred-eighty women together on this tour
Each one, however, on a journey alone.
Roommates were chosen, rooms were assigned;
Groups gathered for walks along the bay.
Sisters met to pray together and work out the kinks
At gospel aerobic sessions early each day.
Sisterly chatter at meals spread the family feel
As repast was shared at tables of eight;
The love was so strong, the excitement so real
Some hardly noticed the food on their plate.
The greetings were friendly and filled with cheer
The hugs for each sister were signs of love,
As each embrace served to spread God's warmth
Through each woman--an extension of His arms from above.
Each woman was alone with an agenda not shared,
Her soul finding its own space in the crowd.
Her countenance signaled to God that she was prepared
While she sang with the praise team out loud.
Each had her secrets, each had her thoughts,
Each snuggled in the lap of the LORD,
Her spirit whispering thanks to God for His grace
As she listened while presenters preached stirring words.
Each met privately with the LORD and got her bearings again
In order to return home as a new woman in God.
Armed with her faith...now renewed, now refreshed,
And awesome memories of His path she had trod.
The parking lot full of family and friends
three buses, luggage, laughter and delight.
Each woman more prepared to follow God's path
having found a more excellent way to His light.

"... We're meeting tonight! Dr Deb is running the meeting! Be there with Christmas articles [and a poem, Toni] on your mind!!! ..."

ADVENT

Luke 2:11

*For unto you
is born this day
in the city of David
a Savior,
which is
Christ the LORD.
(KJV)*

The true shepherd was born in a stable,
Wrapped with linen in the dark of night;
This Advent announced by the angels
A star bathed His manger with light.

*Hope once before and hope once again
The Messiah will come to save us from sin's stain.*

*Peace once before and peace once again
Bathed in God's holy light to salve our earthly pain.*

Matthew 24:50

*The LORD of that
servant shall come
in a day when he
looketh not for him,
and in an hour
that he is not
aware of...
(KJV)*

*Joy once before and joy once again
To set the world right and guide us to God's domain*

*Love since the beginning and love until the end,
This divine Child of Promise...our eternal friend.*

He'll come again wrapped in God's holy light,
To honor a vow made long ago;
This Advent unannounced, unrehearsed,
Just when, even the faithful can't know.

Scriptures Used in This Book

The scriptures used in *Joyfully Enter the Temple: Praise and Meditation Starters* are listed below. Several versions of the Bible were used to provide the scripture selections. Included are the *King James Version, New King James Version, New International Version,* the *Living Bible, New Century Version,* and the *New Living Translation.*

I selected scripture from different versions because I sometimes found that a specific translation was more descriptive, provided more clarity, or more closely matched the tone of the E-mail message than some others. On occasion a certain version simply provided more energy for the piece I was writing.

Acts 1:7-8	*Genesis 24:21*	*Luke 3:5*	*Psalms 40:5*
Acts 2:26-28	*Genesis 28:16*	*Luke 9:35*	*Psalms 42:8*
Acts 4:31-32		*Luke 11:10*	*Psalms 47:1-2*
Acts 5:38-39	*Haggai 2:9*	*Luke 13:22*	*Psalms 61:2-3*
Acts 6:4		*Luke 15:10*	*Psalms 62:1*
Acts 26:18	*Hebrews 4:13*	*Luke 15:20*	*Psalms 88:2*
	Hebrews 12:1-2	*Luke 22:19*	*Psalms 91:11-12*
1 Chronicles 4:9-10		*Luke 22:35*	*Psalms 95:1*
	Isaiah 25:8	*Luke 24:52-53*	*Psalms 95:6*
2 Chronicles 7:14	*Isaiah 40:31*		*Psalms 98:4*
	Isaiah 43:2-3	*Mark 1:35*	*Psalms 98:4-9*
Colossians 3:15, 17	*Isaiah 50:4*	*Mark 4:20*	*Psalms 107:29-30*
	Isaiah 59:17	*Mark 5:28*	*Psalms 119:67*
1 Corinthians 12:31	*Isaiah 61:11*	*Mark 9:22-24*	*Psalms 119:145*
			Psalms 138:3
2 Corinthians 5:16-21	*James 1:6*	*Matthew 4:8-11*	*Psalms 139:1-6*
2 Corinthians 10:14	*James 5:11*	*Matthew 6:8*	*Psalms 143:10*
		Matthew 6:9-15	*Psalms 147:5*
Daniel 2:22	*Jeremiah 1:17*	*Matthew 8:1-2*	
	Jeremiah 17:14	*Matthew 13:43*	*Revelation 15:3*
Deuteronomy 5:33	*Jeremiah 32:17*	*Matthew 22:37-40*	
		Matthew 26:42	*Romans 5:1-5*
Ecclesiastes 9:17	*Job 42:12*	*Matthew 27:46*	*Romans 5:6-9*
		Matthew 28:20	*Romans 8:32*
Ephesians 3:14	*John 3:16*		*Romans 8:28*
Ephesians 3:20	*John 8:25*	*1 Peter 1:8*	*Romans 10:1*
Ephesians 4:29	*John 12:36*	*1 Peter 1:13, 17-20*	*Romans 12:6-7*
	John 14:16	*1 Peter 2:25*	*Romans 14:11*
Exodus 13:18	*John 14:26*		*Romans 15:13*
Exodus 13:21-22	*John 14:19-20*	*Philippians 2:10*	
Exodus 14:13	*John 15:13*		*1 Samuel 1:19*
Exodus 16:7	*John 15:15*	*Proverbs 8:2-3, 6-8*	
Exodus 33:11	*John 15:16*	*Proverbs 22:11*	*1 Thessalonians 4:16*
Exodus 33:14	*John 16:33*	*Proverbs 31:25*	
			1 Timothy 4:6
Ezra 3:11	*Jonah 2:2*	*Psalms 1:3*	
		Psalms 5:3	*2 Timothy 1:6*
Genesis 5:24, 6:9	*Judges 6:15-16*	*Psalms 20:7*	*2 Timothy 1:9*
Genesis 9:9		*Psalms 22:1*	*2 Timothy 2:8-9*
Genesis 9:13	*Lamentations 3:21-23*	*Psalms 26:7*	
Genesis 19:26		*Psalms 34:19*	*Zechariah 3:2*

ORDER INFORMATION

___YES, I want _____ copies of
JOYFULLY ENTER THE TEMPLE
Praise and Meditation Starters
for $12.95 each.

Please include $1.95 shipping and handling for one book,
and $1.00 for each additional book.

Maryland residents must include 5% sales tax.

Name _____

Address _____

City _____ State_____ Zip _____

Phone_____ E-Mail _____

Amount Enclosed $_____

Payment must accompany orders. Allow three weeks for delivery.

Make checks/money orders payable to **T. C. Pearson**.

Send to:

Dove and Turtle Publishing
P.O. Box 44139
Fort Washington, MD 20749

E-mail questions or comments to: **doveandturtle@aol.com.**

ORDER INFORMATION

___YES, I want _____ copies of
JOYFULLY ENTER THE TEMPLE
Praise and Meditation Starters
for $12.95 each.

Please include $1.95 shipping and handling for one book,
and $1.00 for each additional book.

Maryland residents must include 5% sales tax.

Name _____

Address _____

City _____ State_____ Zip _____

Phone_____ E-Mail _____

Amount Enclosed $_____

Payment must accompany orders. Allow three weeks for delivery.

Make checks/money orders payable to **T. C. Pearson**.

Send to:

Dove and Turtle Publishing
P.O. Box 44139
Fort Washington, MD 20749

E-mail questions or comments to: **doveandturtle@aol.co**

It is all so very simple,
Just joyfully enter the temple.

Be blessed!